Preaching the Passion

Interpreting the Evangelists

— GREGORY DUNSTAN —

Sacristy Press

Sacristy Press
PO Box 612, Durham, DH1 9HT

www.sacristy.co.uk

First published in 2022 by Sacristy Press, Durham

Copyright © Gregory Dunstan 2022
The moral rights of the author have been asserted.

All rights reserved, no part of this publication may be reproduced or transmitted in any form or by any means, electronic, mechanical photocopying, documentary, film or in any other format without prior written permission of the publisher.

Scripture quotations, unless otherwise stated, are from the New Revised Standard Version Bible: Anglicized Edition, copyright © 1989, 1995 National Council of the Churches of Christ in the United States of America. Used by permission. All rights reserved worldwide.

Every reasonable effort has been made to trace the copyright holders of material reproduced in this book, but if any have been inadvertently overlooked the publisher would be glad to hear from them.

Sacristy Limited, registered in England & Wales, number 7565667

British Library Cataloguing-in-Publication Data
A catalogue record for the book is available from the British Library

ISBN 978-1-78959-240-5

To the people of St Matthew's Parish Church, Shankill, Belfast,

for whom most of these sermons were written,

*and among whom the author was honoured
to serve the heart of his ministry.*

Contents

Acknowledgments..vi
Preface.. viii

The Passion according to Mark............................... 1
Introduction... 2
1. Preparation at Bethany—The Passion in a nutshell............... 3
2. The supper—The Passion foretold.............................. 6
3. Gethsemane and arrest—The Passion fulfilled................... 9
4. Two trials.. 12
5. Pilate and the soldiers.. 16
6. Crucifixion.. 20
7. Postscript... 23
8. No happy ending 25

The Passion according to Matthew............................ 29
Introduction.. 30
9. Preparation for death... 31
10. Treachery at the table 34
11. Passover fulfilled.. 38
12. Truth and denial... 42
13. Blood sacrifice... 46
14. The Passover of the world 49
15. Raised from the dead.. 51

The Passion according to Luke 55
Introduction 56
16. A last meal together 57
17. Famous last words 61
18. Ultimate failure 64
19. Unexpected friends 67
20. The salvation of the world 70
21. Lord both of the dead and of the living 73

The Passion according to John 77
Introduction 78
22. A preview of the Passion 80
23. The agony 83
24. The death blow 87
25. No greater love 91
26. He gave himself 94
27. Conviction 97
28. The charge 102
29. The witness 106
30. The prisoner 110
31. The judge 114
32. The verdict 117
33. Naming 122
34. Shaming 125
35. Mocking 128
36. Offering 131
37. Piercing 133
38. A burial fit for a king 136
39. Resurrection faith 138
40. The new temple 141

Bibliography 143

Acknowledgments

The preparation of a sermon, or series of sermons, has always begun, for me, with the biblical text, in English and, for the New Testament, in Greek, and one or more commentaries. My first exploration of the Passion according to Mark was with the commentary by Wilfred Harrington, OP (1979). For a first-year theological student, "entry level" it may have been, but its clarity and depth of insight have ensured it a treasured place on my shelves.

For the sermons on Mark and Matthew, I am indebted to the commentaries by Robert H. Gundry (Mark, 1993; Matthew, 1994), whose redaction criticism was particularly helpful to the work in hand. For Mark, I have also consulted from time to time those by Morna Hooker (1991) and D. E. Nineham (1968). For Matthew, I have also used the commentary by John Fenton (1963) and made reference to the magisterial study of the Passion narratives in all four Gospels by Raymond E. Brown, SS, *The Death of the Messiah* (1994).

For the Passion narrative of Luke, I have worked from the commentary by C. F. Evans (1990), supplemented by those of G. B. Caird (1968) and Howard Marshall (1978). For John, my first point of reference has always been C. K. Barrett's commentary on the Greek text (1978), supplemented by the work of John Marsh (1968), Barnabas Lindars, SSF (1972) and, again, Raymond Brown's *The Death of the Messiah*.

Each of the sermons that follow is a personal "reading" of the text, after I have worked through it with the commentators. After twenty centuries of exposition and preaching, there can be very little, if anything, that is new. And yet, each was a personal exploration and interpretation of the text, for a given occasion, and I hope that the reader may find something of help.

I am grateful to Dr Bridget Nichols, the Revd Canon Aonghus Mayes and the Revd Christopher West for reading through some of the first sermons transcribed from my notes and for their suggestions. They gave me the encouragement to proceed.

With their gentle work of editing, Dr Natalie Watson and her team at Sacristy Press completed the transformation of texts prepared for delivery to a volume designed to be read. Theirs is a very particular skill, for which I am grateful indeed.

I have none of his imagination, but must record my debt to my teacher, the late Edwin Owen, Bishop of Limerick and Killaloe. The memory of his example and friendship is an enduring inspiration.

Quotations from scripture are usually from the Anglicized Edition of the *New Revised Standard Version* of the Bible. Sometimes, to highlight a particular emphasis, I have used a translation of my own, checked with other authoritative sources, such as the old *Revised Version* of 1880. Each of these sermons followed the reading of the relevant passage in the context of a service in church. It would, therefore, be helpful to read the passage before exploring each sermon. I hope that these reflections may be helpful, whatever translation of the Bible the reader prefers.

Preface

Most of the sermons in this collection were preached to the congregation of St Matthew's Parish Church, Shankill, Belfast, in Holy Week between the years 2000 and 2005. They mark the journey of rector and people from the evening of Palm Sunday towards Easter. They were "working sermons", researched and written one after another in the course of the week, often with little prior preparation, and amidst whatever urgent pastoral work could not be set aside. Many were subsequently adapted as Holy Week addresses in St Patrick's Cathedral, Armagh. Some were also used as the basis of "Three Hours" devotions on Good Friday.

Each series of sermons was planned and prepared in the belief that the gospel, the Good News of Jesus Christ, is to be heard in the words of the individual evangelists. These, each with his own background, sources, theological outlook and purpose in writing, are the witnesses whom the Church has recognized by its inclusion of their work within the canon of Christian scripture. Scholars may, indeed, seek to go behind their accounts to reconstruct a common ground of events in history with which they are concerned. Such work, however, must inevitably include some element of speculation. Correspondingly, to interpret an incident in one Gospel by reference to an account in another carries a risk of "confusion", of bringing together narratives which may better be distinguished. We do best if we try to interpret the accounts of the four evangelists each in their own terms, in which attention to their specific voices and perspectives, and to the differences between them, may be particularly fruitful and significant.

When first delivered, these sermons made reference to their context in the local community, in Northern Ireland or to events internationally. For the most part, these have been either removed or generalized.

The sermons are presented in the chronological order in which, almost certainly, the Gospels were written, beginning with Mark and finishing with John. This allows the different perspectives of Matthew and Luke to emerge, overlaying as they do the narrative given by Mark. This was not, in fact, the order in which the sermons were written. Because the four Gospels all tell what is, essentially, the same story, there is a degree of repetition between the different series. This is especially so where Matthew follows Mark closely. Luke's account, however, diverges more noticeably from Mark's. Rather than work through Luke's narrative again systematically, I have chosen to highlight those passages in which his account differs. Where there is repetition, I have thought it better to let it stand than to attempt to summarize and cross-reference.

Jesus' Passion is, of course, the climax of all four Gospels. "Jesus Christ and him crucified" (1 Corinthians 2:2) is the heart of the Christian faith. The crucifixion, however, culminated in Jesus' resurrection, without which the story is incomplete. Each series of sermons, therefore, concludes with one (in the case of John, two) on the resurrection as each evangelist portrays it.

Like the Gospels of which they are a part, the Passion narratives were written for and read to Christian congregations. They record an event in history with eternal significance. They both interpret the significance of Jesus' crucifixion, and challenge us to recognize ourselves, our times and society, in the story. That is, they are intended to move us to repentance and faith. The preparation and delivery of these sermons, some of them at the time when we were restoring the parish church, was a significant part of my exploration of the faith. By committing them to print, I hope that they may help others also.

Armagh
The Presentation of Christ in the Temple
2 February 2022

The Passion according to Mark

The Death of the Son of God

Introduction

Like his Gospel, Mark's account of the Passion is the shortest. If, as is probable, the story of Jesus' Passion and death was the earliest part of the gospel story to be remembered consistently among the earliest Christian communities, it was Mark who, as far as we know, first set it down in writing. It is also, of course, to Mark that we owe the very form of a Gospel, an ordered account of the ministry of Jesus in deed and word, as remembered by his followers. If Richard Bauckham is right in reviving the tradition that the evangelist had direct access to the memories of Peter, we have in Mark's narrative of the Passion and in his Gospel as a whole an account as close as we can now get to the life of Jesus himself.*

Probably written for a community of both Jewish and Gentile Christians, shortly before AD 70 and the destruction of Jerusalem's temple by the Romans, Mark's Gospel took shape as the first generation of Christian believers was dying out. Jesus had not returned, as promised, and the Church was suffering persecution. Mark's Gospel has been called "An Apology for the Cross".† It is a call to faith and endurance, to a holding on to truth in the face of disappointment and adversity. Like his Gospel as a whole, Mark's account of the Passion lacks the evident theological overlays of Matthew and Luke, to say nothing of John. Just as, throughout his Gospel, Jesus remains a mysterious figure, challenging both his disciples and the reader to ask, "Who is this?", so Mark's account of the Passion is characterized by enigma and paradox. His "Apology for the Cross" reaches its climax in the one who, betrayed, deserted and denied; subject to a blatant miscarriage of justice; rejected, disowned, abused, violated and crucified is, in all this, revealed as the Son of God and Redeemer of the world.

---

*   Richard Bauckham, *Jesus and the Eyewitnesses: The Gospels as Eyewitness Testimony* (Grand Rapids, MI: Wm. B. Eerdmans, 2006), pp. 155–81.

†   Robert H. Gundry, *Mark: A Commentary on his Apology for the Cross* (Grand Rapids, MI: Wm. B. Eerdmans, 1993).

1

Preparation at Bethany—The Passion in a nutshell

Mark 14:1–11   *Palm Sunday (Evening)*

Jesus' Passion opens, not in Jerusalem but just outside, with a meal interrupted by a visitor. What happens at this meal describes the meaning of the Passion in a nutshell. The scene is framed with menace. Already, Israel's leaders are plotting. Afterwards, Judas joins them. And at the meal itself, everyday values are turned upside down, in a gesture of extraordinary extravagance and in Jesus' interpretation of it. What happens at the meal is a parable of the cross, in which God is at work to achieve his purpose through human actions, both bad and good.

Who was this woman, who intruded into the men's meal together? Mark doesn't say. (Forget, please, the other Gospels: this is Mark, the first to write.) But in she comes, with her ointment in an alabaster jar, carved out of white or translucent limestone, delicate and precious, closed with a stopper. The ointment is nard, most precious of all perfumes, to be treasured and used sparingly. A friend would have been delighted with a finger's touch of it on the forehead. The woman breaks the flask and pours it all over Jesus' head.

The company is outraged. This was a wicked waste: a lovely jar smashed and useless; ointment worth a working man's yearly income dripping down over Jesus' head! Wanton destruction! However this woman came to have such a thing, on any material calculation it would have been better sold and the money given to the poor. Passover was a time for almsgiving. Who they were who so scolded this woman, Mark does not say. They were not necessarily disciples. But their reaction, reflecting prudence, carefulness, a concern for what is fitting and a sense of obligation to the poor, could well be ours.

If those around the table were in any way people like us, Jesus' words are for us no less than for that company. This unknown woman's deed, in all its extravagance, has a quality of its own, and is not to be judged by calculation. The presence of poor people, both within and beyond the Church, must always move us to generosity. And, if giving is to be truly charitable, its only motivation will be concern for them. Our duty to the poor endures as long as poverty exists. Genuine concern for the poor will lead us to discharge our duty, not to use them in argument.

This woman's gesture, however, is of a different order. As kings and priests are anointed on the head, so she has done the same for Jesus. One of Messiah's people has anointed him king. What Jerusalem would refuse, Bethany has done. What the high priest would deny, an anonymous woman has affirmed. What wasn't done in the temple has been enacted in a leper's house. Whatever this woman intended, this is what she has done. Jesus accepts it and re-interprets it. She has anointed his body for burial. Her anointing betokens his impending death. Broken vessel, most precious liquid poured out—her action is in the finest tradition of Israel's prophecy. She is anointing the crucified Messiah, whose death will be in disgrace, his body buried without being embalmed. Only as crucified will Jesus be recognized as Messiah. The good news of the Gospel begins when three other women, going to the tomb to anoint his body, find it empty. Then, what this woman has done will become part of the story. The crowning gesture of an unknown daughter of Israel will be written into the worldwide gospel of God.

In Bethany, a group is gathered around Jesus. In Jerusalem, they are plotting to capture him secretly. They dare not do it at Passover, when Jerusalem is bursting with pilgrims, who are sure to take his side—until Judas goes over to them. Judas, one of the chosen and one of the circle around Jesus, switches sides. Treachery indeed, but the word that we translate as "betray" means, simply, to "hand over". Jesus will be "handed over"—to the priests, to Pilate, to soldiers, to death. But in this "handing over", God is at work—as much as in the unknown woman's anointing. And this "handing over" will take place precisely at Passover, the great feast of Israel's salvation. All through the Passion we trace the will of

God—in the passage of events, in prophetic words and deeds, in Jesus' obedience and in scripture fulfilled—as God gives up his Son to die.

Mark does not say why the woman anointed Jesus, or why Judas betrayed him—only that they did what they did, for in these things is worked out God's will. Judas being "one of the twelve" does, indeed, imply treachery. Even if his motive is hidden from us, Judas' being "one of the twelve" raises the possibility that he may be as representative of them as Peter. Judas in his treachery may be as representative of us as we might wish Peter, in his enthusiasm and humanity, to be. The movement towards Jesus' death had to begin in the circle around him, for this is where God's will is done. Only so was the boundary crossed between enemies and friends. Only so could his enemies, for whom he died, include his friends. All through history, in stained glass and art, Judas has been portrayed as shifty, foxy, dishonest—someone other than us. The truth is that Judas, one of the twelve, could very well be me.

2

The supper—The Passion foretold

Mark 14:12–31   *Monday in Holy Week*

Just as Jesus' anointing at Bethany conveys the meaning of his Passion in a nutshell, so too the Last Supper looks forward to the cross itself. All that happens is a foretelling of the Passion. Jesus is the Messiah recognized in death. In his prediction of betrayal, death, desertion and denial, we already see Good Friday.

We begin with Jesus' foresight of a venue for their Passover. He sends disciples into Jerusalem. They will be met by a man carrying a jar of water. They will follow him to whatever house he goes to and ask, in the Teacher's name, for the guestroom, which the owner will show them. The people of Jerusalem were encouraged to make rooms available for pilgrim families to celebrate Passover; and a man with a jar of water would be an unusual sight. But, says Jesus, he will meet the disciples, not they him. Is this Jesus making arrangements in advance, independent of the twelve, lest he be betrayed? Perhaps. Theologically, however, this is a demonstration of prophetic foresight, almost of Jesus' commanding events. If these predictions are fulfilled, we expect the predictions of his Passion to be fulfilled. If these are fulfilled, the events of Jesus' Passion and death are exactly as he himself foresaw it. His death, in this way, is indeed the will of God. And if this is so, then two further predictions of his that point beyond his Passion will also be fulfilled—of his drinking wine anew in the kingdom of God, and of his going ahead of his disciples into Galilee.*

---

*   For the framework of Jesus' predictions and their fulfilment in his Passion narrative I am indebted to Robert H. Gundry, *Mark* (Grand Rapids, MI: William B. Eerdmans, 1993).

When it comes to the meal, Mark has already told us that Judas will betray Jesus. This, however, is hidden from the rest. Only the traitor knows, and when Jesus speaks of his betrayal, he does not expose him. Rather, he faces the twelve with the terrible truth that one of them will betray him—and this in the context of table fellowship, a shared meal establishing an almost sacred bond. Nor is this any ordinary meal, but Passover, Israel's celebration of her redemption and identity under God. On *this* night Jesus and *his* twelve are gathered, and one of them will betray him.

It could be any one of them. "Surely, not I", they say, all uncertain, each seeking reassurance. Jesus is emphatic: it is one of those dipping in the bowl with him: Psalm 41:9: "Even my bosom friend in whom I trusted, who ate of my bread, has lifted up his heel against me." This is God's will. For Jesus, to expose the traitor would thwart God's will. It would focus the group perhaps violently upon the traitor, not upon him. Jesus is still their shepherd, holding the flock together. But that it should be one of those closest to Jesus is a reminder of the truth that you have to be close to someone to betray them—to know their movements and their mind. The temptation to betray Jesus may be most dangerous for those who are closest to him. Theirs will not be the little slips but failure in what matters most. Those of us who follow him are always at risk of acting from other interests or in service to other powers. So we hand him over to them. Our reasons will be good. Judas had his. But if we do, it would be better for us had we never been born.

After the meal, as they leave for the Mount of Olives, and one slips away in the dark, the pressure does not lift. "You will all desert," says Jesus. "You will all trip on the stumbling block; you will all be ashamed of me. None of you will stay with me." It is a prediction of total failure, all of them little better than traitors. Again, this is God's will: the shepherd will be struck, and the sheep will be scattered (Zechariah 13:7). The flock cannot exist without its shepherd, nor the Church without its Lord.

Peter objects—Peter, the most loyal, the first to have recognized the Messiah (Mark 8:29). Others may fall away—Peter knows his fellow disciples!—but not he. He can stand. Jesus replies with the most specific prediction of all: "Today, this night, before the cock crows twice you will deny me three times." We would like to be strong for Jesus. We despise weakness, and the hero-image appeals. That is make-believe. Had Peter forgotten Jesus' rebuke—"Satan!"—when he had remonstrated with Jesus after his first prediction of his death (Mark 8:31-33)? Even now, after all that Jesus had said, Peter's words suggest that he thought death less probable than his fellow disciples' desertion. Peter's vehemence highlights the all-too-human steps by which he would, indeed, come to deny Jesus. Speaking for himself, Peter is no longer attending to Jesus. There are no Christian supermen. Strength for Jesus is given only through dependence upon Jesus. This is the true faithfulness.

Even in the Supper, there is nothing of comfort. In this Gospel, Jesus says nothing about doing this in memory of him; nothing of the forgiveness of sins. The Supper is the final prediction of his death: "Take; this is my body"—my body, broken, for you; this loaf, taken, blessed, broken, and given, without further explanation. When he gave them the cup, they *all* drank from it—partners with the traitor in his death. This, he said, is "my blood of the covenant, which is poured out for many". The first covenant at Sinai was enacted between God and his people as they were sprinkled with animals' blood. So his death is the sacrifice by which Jesus draws into covenant this guilty, faithless, deserting twelve, and countless more—his life given "a ransom for many" (Mark 10:45). His followers become a people, God's people, by his death, and only by his death. They have no life apart from him.

Mark's is not a comforting Gospel. Mark tells of no subsequent appearance of Jesus, and of only a report of his resurrection. Mark compels us to face the reality of death: of Jesus' death and of every death as the end of the time in which anyone can be known as they are in this life. Whatever it is that may follow, we may never take it for granted. Jesus speaks of his vindication enigmatically in terms of drinking wine anew in the kingdom of God. As raised, he will go before his disciples into Galilee. That is all. The rest is faith. Whatever happens beyond Jesus' death is entirely different from what preceded it. The life of faith, and whatever happens beyond our death, are entirely different from life as we know it. Both depend upon him who was obedient to death—death on a cross.

3

Gethsemane and arrest—
The Passion fulfilled

Mark 14:32–52   *Tuesday in Holy Week*

At the Supper, Jesus had predicted the events of his Passion—betrayal by one of the twelve, desertion by the rest, denial by Peter. In all this is the will of God. As Jesus and his disciples go out to the Mount of Olives, God's will is done.

In the darkness of Gethsemane, Jesus begins at once to separate from his disciples. They are to sit and watch. He goes to pray. He takes with him Peter, James and John, his "three" (an echo of David's "Three"?—2 Samuel 23:8–12). They had witnessed both his raising of Jairus' daughter from death and, on the mountain, his moment of transfiguration. They had seen his glory. He asks them to witness his struggle—a struggle beyond our imagining.

Jesus is distraught, deeply distressed. He is "full of heaviness" (Psalm 42:6), even to death. This struggle is of life and death. He falls before the Father, as once Jairus had fallen before him. He speaks of his hour, the culmination of his mission, and of his cup, his suffering. Jesus faces a death of both calculated and casual violence, with everyone against him, deserted by his own. More terrible still, this is, spiritually, "the last hour". The entire suffering of the last days of the world is focused upon Jesus. God's coming to an ineradicably disobedient world involves a collision of cosmic intensity. All human refusal and rejection of God is concentrated upon Jesus. His is a struggle for the life of the world. Could God not bring in his kingdom in some other way, spare him this cup, this testing? But the world's disobedience can be overcome only by the obedience of him in whom is God's kingdom. Without his obedience, there is no kingdom. There is no alternative. So, "Not my will, but yours". "Your will be done." "Your kingdom come".

Jesus had asked Peter, James and John to watch, to support him in his struggle for the kingdom. Three times he comes and finds them asleep, three times conveying both the intensity of his struggle and their complete failure. By falling asleep they have withdrawn, kept out of it. They couldn't get involved. Peter, so vehement in his loyalty only hours before, Jesus now addresses only as Simon. He is no longer "the Rock", unable even only to watch for one hour. It is an awful moment. "Flesh and blood cannot enter the kingdom of God" (1 Corinthians 15:50). "The spirit indeed is willing, but the flesh is weak." Jesus, possessed by the divine Spirit, is the strong one who struggles. Human spirit is no better than flesh. Jesus' closest three have failed the test. "Lead us not into temptation." "Deliver us from evil."

It comes suddenly, the moment of truth, while disciples sleep: the "hour" of Jesus, the crisis of the world. The Son of Man is handed over to sinners: the man of sovereign freedom surrendered to the selfish interests of common humanity. It begins with betrayal. It must, because unless his own hand him over, a godless world has no power over him. The traitor, Judas, not exposed at the supper, is revealed only in the act of treachery—and with him a gang with swords and clubs sent by "the chief priests, scribes and elders". The full weight of religious authority represented by a mob! "The hands of sinners"! This is devil's work. It will take intimate knowledge to find Jesus in the dark. One word will point him out. A kiss will suffice to identify him. "Rabbi!" Jesus is betrayed with the tenderest greeting of a closest friend. It is the will of God that Jesus be put into the hands of those who would otherwise have no power over him. But there is no evading human responsibility: "It would have been better for that man had he never been born." Judas has secured his place in history and disappears from the gospel of life.

Jesus' protest reveals what is at stake. He is arrested like a bandit—and would be crucified between bandits. They never seized him in the temple. That would have started a riot, with many on his side. To die for "the many", he must be rejected by his own, be treated as a wrongdoer, with no one's sympathy. This is how it must happen. This is God's will. Faced with the power of sinners, his own desert him. The shepherd has been struck. The sheep are scattered. He is on his own.

At the supper, Jesus spoke enigmatically of what would follow his death. He would never again drink wine until he drank it new in the kingdom of God, and, once raised, would go before his scattered flock into Galilee. So too, at this moment, are two signs of God's purpose, even as Jesus is betrayed. As Jesus is arrested, someone with a sword strikes the high priest's servant and cuts off his ear; someone in the crowd, unidentified, unnamed, whatever the later Gospels say. An incident, perhaps, in the heat of the moment. But the high priest's servant represents his master, who sent him. As his slave, he belongs to him. As the shepherd is struck, the high priest's servant is struck. As Jesus is put into his power, and he prepares to try him, his servant is mutilated, and mutilation disqualifies him from office. Only the servant of God stands unblemished.

And who is the young man, following, at the moment of arrest; following when the disciples have fled, naked except for a linen cloth, the same cloth as the shroud in which Jesus would be buried? When his tomb is empty, a young man is found in it, seated, dressed in white. Two young men or one? And if one, who is he? Some suppose the Gospel's author, or perhaps a figure of Jesus himself, Jesus' angel? A figure of him whom death cannot hold, as he slips from his shroud? The figure of one who is still free, even as he is delivered into the hands of sinners? The figure of Jesus who is "The resurrection and the life" (John 11:25)? The figure of Jesus who is the author of the Gospel, who speaks from the tomb to remind his disciples that he is going ahead of them into Galilee?

4

Two trials

Mark 14:53–72　　　　　　　　　　Wednesday in Holy Week

After his betrayal and the desertion of his disciples, all as foretold, Jesus' Passion unfolds. Arrest leads to trial; to two trials simultaneously. Jesus is tried by Israel's leadership, Peter by their servants and followers. Jesus is taken to the high priest, and the whole ruling council is assembled—"chief priests, elders and scribes". The "trial" is rigged from the start: they are "Looking for testimony against Jesus to put him to death". Had he not said (8:31) that he must be rejected by these men and killed? But they find no evidence. There is none. There are no grounds for condemning him. Many, we are told, gave false evidence, but while the law requires the evidence of two or three witnesses to agree, false evidence breaks the eighth commandment—at the heart of Israel's legal code. This trial is self-condemned as a miscarriage of justice.

All sought evidence to put Jesus to death. *Many* gave false evidence. *Some* are specific: "We heard him say, 'I will destroy this sanctuary made with hands, and in three days I will build another not made with hands.'" Surprisingly, however, even on so specific an allegation, their testimony does not agree. To this we will return. But as the trial runs into the sand, the high priest, presiding, takes over the prosecution and invites Jesus to respond to the charges. Jesus is silent. False evidence needs no denial. Jesus will not be condemned for anything alleged against him. Indeed, the evidence of all the false testimony is of his innocence. Jesus is without sin.

So the high priest puts the case directly, using a pious paraphrase for God: "Are you the Messiah, the Son of the Blessed?" For the first time in the whole Gospel, Jesus replies, "I am." Until now he had tried to enforce silence on those who had perceived this. Messiahship could carry all the wrong connotations—of kingship as commonly practised, of glory and power, of resurgent nationalism and political liberation. But now, Jesus is in their hands, destined to die. So he will die as what he is, and as what the Gospel proclaims him to be: "Jesus Christ, the Son of God"—its opening verse; "My Son, the Beloved"—declared at his baptism and at the transfiguration; "The Messiah"—as confessed by Peter (8:29). And, says Jesus, "You will see the Son of Man seated at the right hand of power and coming in the clouds of heaven." So Jesus invokes the authority of scripture—Psalm 110:1 and Daniel 7:13—for his claim to sonship of God and ultimate vindication as Israel's Messiah. Only now, in the certainty of his death, does Jesus make this claim—and so the council that condemns him is judged.

The high priest, however, tears his clothes—down to the skin—names Jesus' response as blasphemy and calls for a verdict. What is the blasphemy? Almost certainly Jesus' claim to the sonship of God, in the sense of an identity and authority grounded in God himself. This the council cannot accept if their own power and position is to be sustained. It cannot concede an overriding divine authority. To preserve the status quo, Jesus is bound to be condemned. So again, the court is judged. As the high priest secures a unanimous conviction and sentence of death, another of Jesus' predictions is fulfilled: "We are going up to Jerusalem, and the Son of Man will be handed over to the chief priests and scribes, and they will condemn him to death; then they will hand him over to the Gentiles; they will mock him, and spit upon him, and flog him, and kill him" (10:33). So here, immediately Mark tells of members of the council spitting on Jesus, hooding him, cuffing him, and calling on him to "prophesy". They demand that he prophesy even as his prophecy is fulfilled! Worse, as Jesus prophesied that the Gentiles would violate him, so here are members of Israel's ruling council behaving like Gentiles. They have condemned their Messiah and have, thereby, implicitly forfeited their place among the chosen people.

Meanwhile, downstairs in the courtyard, another trial is in progress. Peter was sitting with the servants in the warmth of the fire. One of the high priest's maids sees him in its light and accuses him of being with Jesus, the man from Nazareth. Peter feigns ignorance with a double lie: "I neither know nor understand what you're talking about", and slips out into the forecourt. No doubt to Peter's discomfort, the wretched woman follows him, and points him out as "one of them", the group around Jesus, an identification calculated to make Peter feel vulnerable. After further denials, the bystanders, convinced of the accusation, corroborate it: "You're a Galilean." For Peter to curse implies a curse on Jesus. He swears, as if in court, that he does not know him—and the cock crows for the second time. Charged with being with Jesus, or as one of his people, Peter has disavowed Jesus himself. The first disciple called, the first to recognize Jesus as Messiah, has now denied him. The one who promised to die with him, if necessary, could not resist the insinuation of a serving maid. The most committed protestations of loyalty lie in tatters. Jesus' last and most specific prediction has been fulfilled. Peter is broken.

At every stage of the Passion as it unfolds, Mark shows how, through it all, God's purpose is fulfilled. This again, applies to the testimony: "We heard him say, 'I will destroy this sanctuary not made with hands, and in three days I will build another, not made with hands.'" Nowhere else does Mark record Jesus as saying this, but he did predict the destruction of the temple (13:2). On the way into Jerusalem to cleanse the temple, he cursed a fruitless fig tree (11:14) and the next day it was dead. Three times, in predicting his Passion, he spoke of rising on the third day (8:31; 9:31; 10:34). And the temple authorities have been judged even as they condemned him. Readers of the Gospel know that the sanctuary veil was torn at his death, that in three days Jesus was raised by a sovereign act of God, and that henceforth and for ever he is the "place" where God is to be encountered and sin forgiven. By his death he made the temple redundant. The false evidence of his accusers is a prophecy of the truth of Christ.

In the words that sealed his fate, Jesus said, "You will see the Son of Man seated at the right hand of Power and coming in the clouds of heaven." In the very words that will provoke his condemnation, Jesus speaks of his vindication, investiture with the full authority of God, and his exercise of that authority in the ultimate judgement of this world. Jesus had previously spoken of God's kingdom coming in power (9:1), and of "the Son of Man coming in clouds with great power and glory" (13:26). Finally, faced with the certainty of his death, Jesus goes further. His death is itself the key to his exaltation as Lord. Mark says very little about the resurrection, for the things of God, not made with hands, demand the utmost caution. Rather, he sets the transfiguration, the vision of Jesus' glory, at the heart of his Gospel (9:2–8)—and his is the earliest account of it, upon which all others are based—and interprets the ugliness and agony of the cross to help us believe in a crucified Messiah.

5

Pilate and the soldiers

Mark 15:1–20 Thursday in Holy Week—Maundy Thursday

After their night's work, the temple leadership have Jesus bound as a convicted criminal and hand him over to Pilate. If Judas' betrayal of Jesus was, literally, his "handing him over" so the leaders' "handing over" of Jesus to the imperial overlord, to the Gentiles, is no less a betrayal. Where the high priest had asked, "Are you the Messiah, the Son of the Blessed One?", Pilate asks, "Are you the King of the Jews?" To be Messiah is to be king of Israel. Pilate asks the same question, but with contempt for Jesus and his people: "You—are you the king of the Jews?" "Messiah" had political overtones, which Jesus had always avoided. To Pilate, "king of the Jews" has all of those overtones. Pilate represents Rome, empire, racial and cultural superiority, civil law, military power and world government. Pilate is investigating Jesus for sedition, rebellion and treason.

Jesus' reply, "You say so", accepts the title. He could not do otherwise after his answer to the high priest. He accepts the title, but not what Pilate means by it. The temple leadership accuses Jesus of "many things"—presumably of the kind that would make a political charge stick, that would ensure a death sentence. But Jesus is silent, as he was in the face of false testimony at his earlier trial. There is nothing for him to answer; nothing of this nature in the messiahship that is his. His conviction, after all, was on a charge of "blasphemy". There is nothing to the accusations against him.

The custom which Mark reports at this point is one for which there is no other evidence, but which is crucial to what follows: the release of one prisoner at Passover time, at the request of the people. Barabbas is, like Jesus, a prisoner, but a rebel of precisely the kind that the leadership wanted to make Jesus out to be, and a murderer. When the crowd comes to claim the usual custom, Pilate asks only, "Do you want me to release the King of the Jews?" By not offering them Barabbas, Pilate is trying to manipulate Jesus' release. He is also testing the leadership's assertions. If Jesus is the king that they allege, the crowd will come out in his support. Pilate has, indeed, recognized the jealousy behind the leaders' hostility. The title, "The King of the Jews", with its contempt of their nation, is not one that will please the crowd. But in these words Pilate, the representative of imperial authority, proclaims Jesus as Israel's king, her Messiah.

Manipulation, however, is met with manipulation. The leadership "stir up" the crowd to ask for Barabbas—and are thereby shown as the instigators of Jesus' death. So Mark portrays a terrible cynicism in Israel's leadership, asking for the release of a murderer, never mind the sixth commandment. Pilate's reply, "What then shall I do with the King of the Jews?" evokes the response "Crucify him!" This is the first mention in the Passion of crucifixion, a Roman punishment, abhorrent to Jews, here demanded by Jews for a Jew. Crucifixion would have been the fate of Barabbas. Jesus is exchanged for Barabbas; Pilate is to do to Jesus what he would have done to Barabbas. So is established the principle of the cross: our guilt for his innocence, our sin for his righteousness, our shame for his love—as people exchange a murderer for their king.

Pilate could have released Jesus. Once "handed over", however, Jesus is a pawn in a power play. If he releases Jesus, Pilate will have the temple leadership against him, with the possibility of a complaint to Rome. Even had the crowd cried for Jesus, Pilate could not have released him, for its support would have been evidence of a threat to Rome's hegemony. Ever since the moment of betrayal, when Jesus was handed over to his enemies, he has been doomed. Pilate acts politically and amorally. To satisfy both crowd and leaders he releases the guilty and condemns a man whose innocence he has affirmed. As the temple leadership were condemned by their verdict, Pilate is condemned by his decision—and Pilate represents government, politics, the state, law and order as we know them.

"Crucify him!", the two words at the culmination of Pilate's dialogue with the temple leadership, have fuelled Christian anti-Semitism for 2,000 years. To blame the Jewish people for the crucifixion, however, is to ignore and evade our own participation in "the sin of the world", in the systemic structures of selfishness and self-interest—the personal and corporate dimensions of original sin—which infect all social organization and from which no one is exempt. The disciples, our spiritual ancestors, were Jews. One—a representative one—handed Jesus over. Three were unable to support Jesus in his spiritual crisis. All but one ran away when the going got tough, and the one who didn't—the leader—explicitly denied his Master. None of us is without our place somewhere in this story. The Jewish people, too, are the archetypal religious people, deriving their community and identity from God, and it is typical of religious people like us to hold on to what we have, and to God as we understand him and have made him, failing to recognize the fullness of freedom and life that God offers.

On the evening of Maundy Thursday, as whenever they celebrate the Eucharist, Christians repeat the words that Jesus used to predict his death—having told those with him around the table that one of them would betray him. He did not, according to Mark, say who. It could be any one of them, as they realized. When he gave them the cup they all drank from it—and the traitor was part of the fellowship. So too we all drink from the cup and betray our Lord into the hands of sinners. While taking his name, and claiming citizenship of his kingdom, we live by laws and standards other than his. So we make him the prisoner of our political arrangements and social order. We subject him to our economic systems and the demands of our lifestyle. We keep him shut up in our churches and bind him to our ways of thinking. We are all guilty of the body and blood of our Lord (1 Corinthians 11:27ff.). But only as guilty can we be forgiven; this is the gift of the exchange.

Once he is condemned, the soldiers take Jesus into their headquarters' courtyard and summon the rest. They clothe him in purple, like their emperor. They weave a crown of "thorns",* like the bay-leaves worn by

---

* European sensibility since medieval times has seen the "crown of thorns" as viciously spiked, painful and drawing blood, as if made of blackthorn or buckthorn. Buckthorn is, indeed, possible, but the word in the Greek of all the Gospels most naturally indicates the Acanthus plant, known in English as "Bear's Breeches", whose long, fleshy leaves are the ornamentation on a Corinthian capital, and would have been readily twisted into a parody of Caesar's bay-laurel crown.

Caesar in the triumph of victory. Instead of "Hail, Caesar!" they cry, "Hail, King of the Jews!", with all their contempt for a people whom they despise. They strike the crowned head with a floppy reed. They spit on the kingly robe.

In all this, Jesus' words are fulfilled, that he would be handed over to the Gentiles, who would mock him, spit upon him, flog him and kill him (10:34). But they needn't have done all this. A barrack-room roughing-up could well have been normal but, like the false testimony against Jesus before the high priest, this ghastly parody points beyond itself. This is the governor's courtyard, with the whole battalion assembled. Jesus is robed in imperial purple and crowned. He is acclaimed, "King of the Jews!". He is "worshipped", which is what the word for homage means, by Gentile soldiers, people like us. Handed over to them, they will crucify him. So he will die for them as he will die for those who demanded his crucifixion, and for those who betrayed, deserted and denied him: the innocent for the guilty. Such is the principle of exchange. Crucified, Jesus will be recognized as their Lord and ours, the Christ, the Anointed One, the Messiah of Israel and the Saviour of the world.

6

Crucifixion

Mark 15:21–39   *Good Friday*

Jesus' crucifixion brings to fulfilment all that has preceded it in the story of his Passion, and, indeed, in the entire Gospel. The threads of all that has gone before are drawn together. Offered wine sweetened with myrrh, Jesus refuses it. Had he not said that he would not again drink wine until he drank it anew in the kingdom of God? The testimony about his destroying the sanctuary and building it in three days, given at his trial, is repeated, and the sanctuary veil is torn as he dies. At his death, the centurion confesses as true what the high priest had denied—Jesus, the Son of God. And throughout there are echoes of scripture: three references to Psalm 22, one to Psalm 69, others to Isaiah 53. Jesus dies "according to the scriptures": his death is the fulfilment of the purposes of God, for the salvation of the world.

    Mark doesn't go into details about Jesus' crucifixion. There was no need to do so. It was familiar to his hearers. Mark is concerned with words. What was begun at Gethsemane (meaning "oil press", on the Mount of Olives) is finished at Golgotha, "The place of a skull". Jesus was crucified as "King of the Jews", the title Pilate gave him, the king rejected by his own; the king mocked by Gentile soldiers; the king crucified between two bandits—the king proclaimed innocent amid the guilty. Once Jesus is crucified, there begins a three-fold mockery—as three times Jesus foretold his Passion, three times he prayed in the garden, three times he found his disciples asleep, and three times Peter denied him. The passers-by repeat the allegation of Jesus destroying the temple and building it in three days—for the temple is the symbol of their national identity as God's people. The leaders of the temple gloat among themselves. The demand that Jesus "come down from the cross" is the old demand for a sign, by those who cannot or will not see. (Is this, again, why Mark says nothing of anyone seeing Jesus after his resurrection—because to see is not, in fact, to believe (John 20:29)?) Jesus' co-crucified also taunt him. Jesus dies alone, with the venom of his own people heaped upon him. He cannot save himself. Only God can save, and God cannot save him. He has been handed over; delivered into the power of politically self-centred humanity. God's people behave like Gentiles. This is what we all do.

Death comes quickly, in six hours. This is unusual: the crucified usually died, quietly, on the third day. Was it because Jesus was already weakened that they compelled Simon of Cyrene to carry his cross? (His name recalls, of course, another Simon, who slept, and then disowned his Lord. But this Simon and his sons were known to Mark's community; the first of a new generation of disciples who was turned back from the way he was going, to take up the cross and follow him.) Weakness alone, however, cannot account for all that happened. With the sun at midday, darkness descended on the whole land—even the whole earth—for three hours. This is an event of cosmic significance. One who calmed the storm, and walked upon water, who fed five thousand, and four ... now hangs upon a cross.

After three hours of darkness, Jesus cries with a loud voice. The crucified usually groan and whisper—it's all that they can do. But Jesus is wrestling with death itself. *"Eloi, Eloi, lema sabachthani?"* (Psalm 22:1). Jesus is abandoned, forsaken; abandoned by God, deserted even by the Father, his "Abba". He is given up to death, but in his abandonment cries out as one who is, even now, doing God's will. In this ultimate extremity, this rupture of the godhead, the sinless exchanged for the sinful, the embodiment of God for sordid humanity, is achieved the redemption of the world.

Jesus' cry is loud enough for the bystanders to hear—and to mistake *"Eloi"* for Elijah—Elijah who was supposed to come to the aid of the righteous in their tribulation; Elijah, with whom Jesus had spoken on the mountain; Elijah, who was supposed to come before the End. But Elijah doesn't come. Elijah had already come—as Jesus had said (9:13). This is the End. Another great shout, and Jesus dies—or, rather, in that shout, Jesus dies, with immediate consequence both for Israel and the world. The veil of the temple is torn in two from top to bottom; the veil covering the entrance to the sanctuary, the place of God's presence. "I will destroy this sanctuary ... " they had alleged against Jesus—and it is done. The temple's day is over. God is no longer so confined. Israel's privilege as God's uniquely chosen people is at an end. A new sanctuary is in process of building ... And, as Jesus dies, the centurion recognizes in him "a son of God". What he, a Gentile, a pagan, a soldier, a sinner meant by that, only he knew. But he is the first of the pagan world—our world—to see something never seen before. In Jesus, crucified, he sees him whom Mark (1:1) proclaims, "Jesus Christ, the Son of God".

In that final shout, as Jesus died, to translate literally Mark's Greek, he "ex-spirited". What was begun at his baptism was completed in his death. At the beginning, the Spirit was given. At the End, he sent it forth. At the beginning the heavens were torn apart. At the end the sanctuary veil was torn in two. At the beginning the voice of God proclaimed his Son, the Beloved. At the end, his own voice cries out God-forsaken—and the voice of a soldier proclaims him Son of God. Jesus, rejected by the righteous, is recognized by the man who crucified him; by the first of the sinners for whom he gave his life, a ransom for many.

7

Postscript

Mark 10:35–42; 15:27

Mark's account of Jesus' Passion shows its outworking according to his own prediction and in fulfilment of scripture. There is, however, one further "fulfilment" even if it is an insight of the evangelist rather than of Jesus himself.

Not long before Jesus and his disciples arrived in Jerusalem, and immediately after his third prediction of his Passion, James and John asked that they might sit, one at Jesus' right hand and one at his left, in his "glory" (10:37). In reply, Jesus asks if they can share his suffering, and they affirm that they can. Jesus then tells them that they will, indeed, share his suffering, but that, "to sit at my right hand or at my left is not mine to grant, but it is for those for whom it has been prepared". In his reply, in Mark's Greek, Jesus uses a euphemism for the word, "left"—literally, "well-named" (10:40). When Jesus is crucified, with him are two bandits, "one on his right and one on his left". For "left", Mark again uses the euphemism (15:27). For comparison, Matthew uses the euphemism on all three occasions (Matthew 20:21,23; 27:38).

It is hard to escape the conclusion that, by first changing to the euphemism on Jesus' lips, and then using it of one of those crucified with him, Mark is making a point. Those who will share most intimately in Jesus' glory are those crucified with him. If so, it is, indeed, "scandalous". This is contrary to every human notion of what is just and deserving. Those who were crucified with Jesus were robbers, brigands or bandits; outlaws condemned to death. They joined in the taunting and mockery of Jesus even as they hung there beside him. They were among his enemies to the end. But Mark shows here the totality of the redemption wrought by Jesus; the extent of his "ransom for many" (10:45). Those who were crucified with Jesus were the first to die with him; the first, indeed, to share the baptism with which he was baptized (10:39). This is the immensity of the divine love. If this is so, none of us, surely, is beyond the compass of Jesus' death.

In the similar passage in Matthew's Gospel, Jesus says that to sit at his right hand and at his left is not his to grant, "but it is for those for whom it has been prepared by my Father" (20:23). So Matthew, characteristically, reserves the issue, which is one of judgement, to the will of God. Luke, with the emphasis on repentance characteristic of his Gospel, picks up something of Mark's insight. In his account, one of Jesus' co-crucified joins in the taunting. The other "rebukes" him, recognizes his own wrongdoing and Jesus' innocence, and asks Jesus to remember him when he comes "into his kingdom". He is met with the promise, "today, you will be with me in Paradise"—the first, surely, to share in the salvation of which Jesus is the author (Luke 23:39–43).

By incorporating the repentance of one of those crucified with Jesus, Luke also aligns the differing fates of the two bandits, as presumably he saw them, with another of his themes: the cross as the place both of salvation and of judgement—the opposite sides of the same coin. Mark's vision is bolder, more terrible. Dying God-forsaken and utterly alone, Jesus has borne the judgement. In him, henceforth, there is only salvation. Those who died with him, even as those who are among his enemies, are exalted with him. This leaves, of course, the issue of those whose lives, on any reckoning, have, and to elaborate no further, brought suffering, misery and death to others. We are back to the "scandal" of Mark's insight. But this is the point. Even to raise the issue is to assume something at least of the role of judge, and of making distinctions which, however apparent to us, may be less evident, to say the least, in God's sight. This also leaves unresolved the fate of Judas. Unlike Matthew and Luke, who record respectively his suicide and death, Mark says nothing further of him. "It would be better for that one not to have been born," said Jesus at the supper. Could it be that Jesus' death ultimately redeems even this? Perhaps we should hope that it does, for there are very few of us who have not at some stage betrayed our Lord.

8

No happy ending

1 Corinthians 15:1–11; Mark 16:1–8   Easter Day

> Angels in bright raiment rolled the stone away,
> kept the folded graveclothes where thy body lay . . .
> Lo, Jesus meets us, risen from the tomb,
> lovingly he greets us, scatters fear and gloom.
> *Edmond Budry (1854–1932), transl. R. B. Hoyle (1875–1939)*

So we sing—but not according to the Gospel of Mark. He tells of three women going to Jesus' tomb two days after his burial. In the first light of the risen sun, they see the stone already rolled away. In the tomb, there is nothing to see, except a mysterious young man who gives them a message for the disciples. They flee, terrified. They don't see Jesus. They don't tell anyone.

This is how Mark finished his Gospel. No "happy ending". The hymn quotes details from the other Gospels for, ever since Mark, people have thought that he should have said more. The later evangelists do. Others added to Mark's Gospel what they thought he should have said. Some scholars think Mark said more, but that the text got lost. But these last verses of Mark's Gospel make perfectly good sense as they are. Mark finished his Gospel with three women, running, saying nothing to anyone—and as Mark's is the first account that we have of the empty tomb, we should pay attention.

Everybody knew that the risen Christ had appeared to his disciples. This is the earliest Christian tradition. Paul says, "Christ died for our sins according to the scriptures; he was buried; he was raised on the third day in accordance with the scriptures." He appeared to Peter, to the twelve, to

25

more than five hundred, to James, to all the apostles, and finally to Paul, the only one to witness to the fact in writing (1 Corinthians 15:3-8). Nor is there any doubt about what Mark believed (9:9). He entitles his book, "The Gospel of Jesus Christ the Son of God". He wrote it as a Gospel of the crucified Christ. He is uncompromising about the resurrection. But the church for which he wrote was struggling. Nearly forty years on, the eyewitnesses of Jesus were dying out. He hadn't returned as they had all expected. Emperor Nero was persecuting Christians. The church needed not a happy ending but a call to faith.

Mark tells of three women coming to honour Jesus' body with an anointing fit for a king—spices, not oils. The stone, too heavy to shift, has been moved. Inside the tomb, instead of a corpse, wound in linen—perhaps brown, unbleached—is a young man sitting on the right, sitting where Mark's church confesses Jesus to be, where Jesus has said he would be (14:62), at the right hand of God; and the young man is robed in white—as at Jesus' transfiguration. This man is an angel: Jesus' angel, Jesus' representative and messenger. The women are overwhelmed.

In the Gospel, these women alone follow Jesus to his death and burial. In the strongest possible terms, the angel tells them that the Jesus they're looking for, the crucified, has been raised from the dead. The body taken lifeless from the cross has been raised. "He is not here." Nor has Jesus gone on to immortality, leaving his body behind. He has been raised. And his message for the disciples repeats Jesus' last words to them all as they set out for Gethsemane. They would all desert him, "but after I am raised up, I will go before you into Galilee" (14:28). There they will see him. Not here, now, but in Galilee.

But the message didn't get through. "They said nothing to anyone." The women, the only witnesses to Jesus' cross, burial and resurrection, proved in the end no more reliable than the disciples. And, if the message didn't get through, Mark could not tell us about the disciples seeing Jesus in Galilee. But everybody knew, Mark included, that the disciples did see Jesus. This was at the heart of the Gospel. The point is that Jesus' appearances are not an explanation of an empty tomb—one explanation among other possibilities. Jesus' appearances are the sovereign activity of one raised to the throne of God. His resurrection is without precedent, radically new, nothing less than the beginning of a new creation. The old ways of seeing don't matter anymore. What matters now is faith, and faith is only possible in the risen, glorified Christ. The women's failure to pass on the message marks, in fact, a new beginning.

The angel is Jesus' messenger, but his voice is Mark's. His message is the message of the Gospel and of its ultimate author, Jesus Christ, the Lord of the Church, sitting at the right hand of God. He is not now to be seen by human sight. His sovereignty is universal. The message is for us, his disciples who have denied or deserted him. He is going ahead of us into Galilee. Why Galilee? At the beginning of his Gospel, after the baptism and temptation, Mark writes, "Jesus came into Galilee, proclaiming the Gospel of God" (1:14). Later, at the heart of the Gospel, when Peter has recognized Jesus as the Messiah, when Jesus has first predicted his death and just before his transfiguration, Jesus says, "There are some standing here who will not taste death until they see that the kingdom of God has come with power" (9:1). As Galilee, beside the little sea, is where Jesus first declared the kingdom of God, so here it is. Galilee is now global. Galilee is wherever God's kingdom is proclaimed, where his disciples proclaim Jesus' sovereignty. And wherever Jesus' sovereignty is proclaimed we may expect to "see" him doing what first did in Galilee, calling disciples, confronting evil, healing the sick, cleansing the unclean, including the outcast, forgiving sins, sowing the word of the kingdom—and raising the dead. If it ever seems to us that we do these things, it is in fact Jesus himself, as he goes ahead of us in sovereign power. But in doing these things we shall see him at work in changed lives and in the changed world that bears witness to the kingdom of God.

The Passion according to Matthew

Passion and Passover

Introduction

Matthew's is the most explicitly Jewish of the four Gospels. Jesus stands in the shoes of Moses. Jesus is the new lawgiver, with the "Sermon on the Mount" and four other passages of teaching worked into the narrative framework laid down by Mark, together reminiscent of the five Books of Moses, the Torah, the Law or, more properly, the "Teaching". As Jesus is the Teacher, so Matthew's Gospel emphasizes discipleship, the following of Jesus. Jesus speaks and acts with sovereign authority, as Israel's Messiah. A theme that runs throughout the Gospel is the fulfilment of scripture, the Law and the Prophets in Jesus, in what he says and does. Jesus' status as Israel's Messiah was, no doubt, the central issue between Matthew's church and the Jewish community from which it had separated, which denied this as strongly as the Church affirmed it. This gives rise to a polemic which has found its way into the Passion narrative itself.

The foundation of Israel's existence as a people was and is the nation's deliverance from slavery in Egypt, commemorated annually at Passover. As Jesus was crucified at Passover, so Matthew's Gospel shows his death as the fulfilment of all that Passover meant, but now for all the peoples of the world. Jesus' death fulfils Israel's entire history, God's whole purpose for his chosen people, as expressed in the scriptures. Throughout the Passion story, Jesus' sovereignty is expressed and affirmed, even in the violence and abuse of all that is done to him. Through his death is inaugurated what he proclaimed, with characteristically Jewish paraphrase, "the kingdom of heaven". Raised to nothing less than the full authority of God (28:18), Jesus sends his disciples to make more disciples, in accordance with this Gospel.

9

Preparation for death

Matthew 26:1–16 *Palm Sunday (evening)*

Two days before Passover: a time for preparation, not for Passover itself but for something that would transform the national festival of Israel into the turning point of the history of the world. So, in Jerusalem, they gathered at the high priest's palace. Two miles away friends gathered for a meal. A gathering of the great and the good, hosted by Caiaphas; a gathering of a bunch of nobodies hosted by Simon the leper. But one of the nobodies went over to the great and the good and made a name for himself: Judas Iscariot.

The great and the good were the aristocracy of Israel, chief priests and elders, the leaders of the people of God. To them, Jesus was a threat. He had challenged their powerbase in the temple. He was popular with the people. He taught the imminence of the kingdom of God. Some spoke of him as the Messiah, the Lord of that kingdom. The great and the good act politically: no dialogue, no prayerful discussion, no common search for truth. Like ruling elites the world over, they defend their position, a lonely position, unsupported by the people thronging Jerusalem for Passover. The established order has everything to lose from Jesus' gospel of good news for the poor; his including of those whom the system excludes; his friendship with the unacceptable. If God's kingdom is like this, position and privilege have no place. They act accordingly.

Had Jesus been recognized as king, the high priest would have anointed his head with oil in the temple—a symbol of his divine authority and of the Spirit's gifts to rule. Jesus comes with the authority of his birth, of his identification with his people in baptism by John, and of the Spirit's anointing. But something is still missing and it is supplied by a nameless woman in the house of Simon the leper. Jesus is anointed by one of his own. Instead of a plot, an act of homage. Instead of life taken, a costly gift. Did she know what she was doing? Or has God's Spirit made her a prophet, made of her love a deed whose significance she had never realized? Jesus accepts her anointing, but as signifying his burial. His kingship is exercised only in death. He came, Jesus, Immanuel, God with us, "to save his people from their sins" (1:21). This means to die for them. He came to bring in God's kingdom. That involves a universal presence. Jesus can reign only through death and resurrection. Even as Caiaphas plots and Judas betrays, God's will is done.

Did Judas see nothing in this? The contrast with his treachery could not be sharper. The woman honoured Jesus as her Lord; Judas renounced his sovereignty. The woman made Jesus a gift; Judas asked for money and was given thirty shekels (Zechariah 11:12)—five months' wages. It was a lot to Judas, nothing to those who gave it to him to buy the arrest of the man who lodged with Simon the leper. God or money; love or money? This is our choice—the choice as Jesus put it, the choice as the woman made it, the choice as Judas made it, the choice before us all.

This is where we come in, as followers of Jesus. Those disciples recognized the cost of the ointment. Poor themselves, they knew the value of money, and what that money could do. They recognized their duty to the poor. They were not wholly wrong in their criticism. But neither were they right, for love trumps calculation. A gift in love is never wasted. Unable to see the gesture for what it is, they condemn the anointing of their Master and Messiah as "a waste". They have not recognized Israel's king, and his kingdom. They have not recognized the significance of this moment, this moment in history, for which he had tried to prepare them, of which he had spoken so many times. Yes, the poor are always with us. So where is our heart? Church people tend to be good with money. But where are we between love and calculation, between God and money, between an unknown woman and Judas Iscariot, between Jesus and Caiaphas? Get this right, and everything else will fall into place.

Since that moment when Peter first recognized him as Israel's Messiah (16:16), Jesus had three times predicted his Passion (16:21; 17:22-23; 20:18-19). Now, at Passover, the time has come—and still Jesus tries to prepare his disciples. Passion and Passover go together. Passover celebrates Israel's salvation, the death of Egypt's firstborn as a lamb was sacrificed, and God's constituting Israel as his people. Passover also celebrates Israel's hope, of God's redeeming his people again, reconstituting the nation as he gathers in her exiles. So, to this Passover comes Israel's king. At this Passover God's firstborn will die—to gather in the exiles, to welcome the excluded, to enact a new covenant for the forgiveness of sins. This covenant will be without limit. This Passover will be celebrated for the salvation of the world.

10

Treachery at the table

Matthew 26:17–35 *Monday in Holy Week*

Passion and Passover are intimately connected. Passover celebrated Israel's redemption from Egypt, and her hope of salvation to come. Jesus' Passion transformed the redemption and hope of Israel into God's gift and promise to the world. Matthew's account of the Passion explores this connection. The story he tells he took from Mark, but he tells it differently. To see, therefore, how Matthew understood the significance of Jesus' death and resurrection means exploring especially the differences: what Matthew adds, what he leaves out, what he rephrases, and why.

This part of the story concerns the Passover meal, in two parts, each introduced by the phrase, "While they were eating". So Jesus' prediction that Judas would betray him sets the context of what he would do with bread and wine. And his commandment regarding the bread and wine is in the context of his certain death. Before this, we hear of the preparation of the Passover. Afterwards we hear of desertion and denial of Jesus by his disciples, as the working out of the Passion begins.

Matthew tells of preparing the Passover very simply. Gone is the mystery of Mark's account—of two disciples sent to follow a man with a water jar and finding a guest room already prepared. In Matthew's account, Jesus' disciples ask where they should prepare for *him* to eat the Passover, and he sends them off to do it. This, therefore, is *Jesus'* Passover. He invites himself into a house to eat it—literally, to "make" it—with his disciples. He knows of the priests' plot and of Judas' betrayal. His time is at hand, as he had from the beginning proclaimed the kingdom of God at hand. This Passover will be his Passion. His Passion will fulfil Passover, and through Passover his Passion will be remembered for generations to come. Jesus' disciples, then, preparing for Passover, foreshow the Church preparing for worship. Jesus invites himself to a house. All present are involved and do as he tells them with bread and wine.

But before Jesus takes the bread and wine, he sets what he will do in the context of his death: of betrayal by one of his own. Again, the first impetus to Jesus' death came from within the circle, from among his disciples, from one of us. All the Gospels connect the betrayal with the table fellowship of the Passover. In Mark's account, the traitor could be any one of them around the table. Matthew distinguishes the traitor from the rest. Judas, we know, is already in the pay of Jesus' enemies. Betrayal, then, is not something that disciples can do. If they do it, they cease to be disciples. Where the Church is suffering persecution, as Matthew's was, betrayal is an ever-present possibility. How should any of us stand where Christians must meet in secret today? The disciples' anxious, "Surely not I, Lord?" bespeaks the danger for us all. It would have been better for the traitor never to have been born. It is a most terrible warning. Judas has dipped with Jesus in the dish—has been intimately identified with him as their fingers touched. Betrayal is by an intimate friend. And *his* question is different from the others', "Surely not I, *Rabbi*?"—a title of honour, but not the title of Lord. Judas has renounced Jesus' sovereignty. If Jesus is our Lord, who commands our obedience, we will not betray him. If he is something less, we may—and perhaps we will.

When it comes to the bread and the wine, Matthew's account of the Passover is unique in that Jesus specifically commands his disciples both to eat the bread of his body and to drink the cup of his blood. This is at once the language of sacrifice, of a meal and of covenant: of sacrifice, because the victim was eaten and its blood poured out; of a meal, because bread and wine are consumed; and of covenant because, in the making of a covenant, blood was sprinkled upon the parties, upon the altar of the Lord and upon the people. We call this the Supper. Matthew calls it the Passover, the event which it was, which Jesus told his disciples to prepare, and which he commands them to do.

Why? First, because, "this is my blood of the covenant, poured out for many for the forgiveness of sins". He does not call this a new covenant. "My blood of the covenant" recalls God's covenant with Israel at Sinai, which still stands. Jesus' blood-shedding is in continuity with and in re-affirmation of that covenant, even as he expands its reach from Israel to the world. Second, there is the Passover Lamb, whose blood on the doorposts and lintels of the Israelites' homes spared their firstborn from the death visited upon Egypt. So here, God's Firstborn gives his blood for the sins of his people. But, third, Jeremiah spoke of a new covenant involving the forgiveness of sins (Jeremiah 31:31–34). This is it: "my blood of the covenant, poured out for many for the forgiveness of sins". This is the heart of the covenant in Jesus. This is why it is new, and is unlimited in its reach, a covenant "for many", for all humanity. In this is fulfilled the name of Jesus, who "will save his people from their sins" (1:21). In this way, Jesus declares his Passover to be of universal significance. We eat and drink because his Passover ever presents and re-presents his death. Not to do so would be to neglect Jesus' explicit command.

And there is more. Jesus would never again drink of the fruit of the vine until he drank it new with his disciples in his Father's kingdom. So again, Jesus prophesies his death, and his death as the inauguration of God's kingdom. He reigns as Messiah only in death. But his words are also an assurance to his disciples of their participation in that kingdom. They will drink with him in it. They are also an assurance of his presence with us in the kingdom. Our eating and drinking are an anticipation of our presence with him, in his Father's kingdom, and an assurance of his presence (1:23) with us now.

Matthew, as we saw, dissociates Judas from the disciples—but not Peter. When Jesus foretells their desertion, he is included with the others, and his protestations of loyalty, even to death, are echoed by theirs. Disciples may not betray one another and remain disciples. Disciples must not break the covenant of love; but they may indeed desert their Lord. Jesus dies for us in our weakness and failure, as much as for those who know nothing of him. He dies for the forgiveness of sin, our own no less than anyone else's. The shepherd will be struck; the sheep will be scattered. But, risen, he will go ahead of them into Galilee—Galilee of the Gentiles (4:15)—gathering them again out of all the nations of the earth.

Peter's inability—and ours—to stand with Jesus is more than a failure of human courage. True, his pledge to stand should others fail was unwise. Comparison is dangerous. Peter does recognize, too, that faithfulness to

Jesus may lead to death. But Peter's "even though I must die with you, I will not deny you" suggests that, even now, he has recognized neither the necessity of Jesus' death nor its utter loneliness. Jesus is saying that no one can stand with him: all will be deserters, and Peter, by cockcrow, will have achieved no more than those who ran away at the beginning. Jesus is taking on more than any human being can. Jesus is involved in confronting sin, the sin in which all are involved and enmeshed. Jesus is taking on the sin of the world, embodied in all its institutions and ways of life: in religion, in politics, in nation and society, in commerce and trade, in law and learning, in every exercise of power, in the dynamics of the crowd and in the human heart. This is why he came. This is why he was named "Jesus". This is the heart of God's covenant in him. "This is my blood of the covenant, which is poured out for many for the forgiveness of sins."

11

Passover fulfilled

Matthew 26:36–56　　　　　　　　　　Tuesday in Holy Week

As Jesus and his disciples finished their Passover together and went to the Mount of Olives, Jesus foretold their desertion. His word means more than their abandoning him. They would all be offended, scandalized and fall into sin because of him. Almost immediately his words are fulfilled. In Gethsemane his Passover continues, not in a meal, but in what happens. Jesus' Passion is his Passover. In Gethsemane we see its cost: we see the witness of three disciples to Jesus' obedience, even as they fail him, and we see fulfilled his predictions of his betrayal and their scattering as Judas re-appears.

Far from softening Mark's account of Jesus' anguish, Matthew fills it out: three hours, three episodes of prayer, while his disciples in their sleep already desert him. His "soul is deeply troubled, even to death" (Psalm 42:5,11; 43:5). Jesus falls on his face. He is overwhelmed. His words to the three to "remain here" while he goes on recall Abraham's instructions to his servants as he and his son went on to the place of sacrifice (Genesis 22:5). He prays about a cup. At the supper, he had commanded them all to drink from the cup. In the Hebrew scriptures, the cup is a figure of destiny, of joy or of suffering. Would James and John be able to drink of his cup (20:22)? But now Jesus pleads with his Father that, if possible, this cup pass from him. The word "pass" is that used for the Lord's passing through Egypt to strike its firstborn (Exodus 12:12). Jesus is praying to be spared his Passover, to be spared as the sacrifice, as Isaac was; to be spared as the victim, the lamb whose blood was smeared over the doorframes of the Israelites in Egypt; to be spared as the sacrifice whose blood is poured out for the forgiveness of sins. Jesus is praying to be spared the burden of the sin of the world. The second time, however, as he prays, he says, "Father if this cannot *pass* unless I drink it, your will be done." The third time he prays the same. As three times he was tempted and was obedient (4:1-11), so three times Jesus prays and is obedient. Jesus will go through with his Passover. He is our Passover, sacrificed for us (1 Corinthians 5:7). It is the cup of his blood that we share in the Eucharist. Because he has been obedient, and drunk the cup of suffering, it is for us "The cup of pardon, healing, gladness, strength".*

Jesus' anguish is attested by three disciples, Peter, James and John, three of the first four chosen (4:18-22). They had been granted the vision of his glory—his raising of Jairus' daughter and his transfiguration on the mountain. Here, as on the mountain, they sleep, but, as then, they see what they must, his obedience to death. So Jesus prays, that second time, as he had taught them to pray, "Your will be done." Jesus prays as he taught, and dies as he prays, and it is through his death that he enters his glory. Jesus reigns only as the crucified Messiah. Jesus' obedience is the central dynamic of his crucifixion. Jesus endures where Adam failed. "A second Adam to the fight and to the rescue came."† His obedience is for us all. This is the essence of his Passover.

Jesus had asked Peter, James and John to watch, to stay awake with him. (Just as his words to Peter are addressed to all three, so, when Matthew speaks of the disciples, they stand for us all.) But they could not. Whether it was the wine of the meal, the night, weariness or a psychological avoidance of the struggle, the Gospel does not say. Rather, it records their failure to watch and pray so that, when they are tested, they fail. In fact, they act in our common humanity, "sleeping and taking their rest" at night, as we all do, and need to do. *This* is the point. This struggle is of flesh against Spirit. In the three, the flesh wins, and they fail. In Jesus, the Spirit wins, and he is obedient to death. Jesus is obedient where we, without him, fail. And their failure to pray is directly related to their desertion, as Jesus had foretold.

---

*   From a prayer of preparation for the Eucharist in Eric Milner-White, *My God, my Glory* (London: SPCK, 1954), p. 70.

†   John Henry Newman: "Praise to the Holiest in the Height", from *The Dream of Gerontius*.

This is of more than historical significance. Three times Jesus comes to them. Jesus is "The Coming One". His instruction to us as disciples is to watch and pray lest we enter into temptation—another echo of his prayer. Our time of trial and tribulation may be the time of our judgement, when he comes to us, be it the trial of persecution, apostasy, carelessness, indifference, drift or our absorption by one of the ideologies of this age. Unless we stay with him, watch and pray with him, we are weak, hopelessly weak. If we are preoccupied with "keeping the show on the road", even if that "show" is the church, we too are asleep in the garden. Christians should note how our Muslim brothers and sisters pray—four times daily. Christians of more accommodating lifestyles should note how others of more demanding traditions pray, whether from a deeply inherited devotion or the energy of personal commitment: Morning Prayer, Evening Prayer—and a midday prayer too; "The Jesus Prayer", silent prayer, scriptural meditation, *Lectio Divina*, arrow prayers, grace before meals, prayers at the kitchen sink; all brought together in the Eucharist and the corporate prayer of Christ's people.

Suddenly, Judas arrives. Jesus' "hour" has come. As he said when he sent them to prepare his Passover, "My time is at hand" (26:18). Judas has come with a crowd wielding the weapons of this world. What Jesus has foretold is played out: "One of the twelve"; "the betrayer"; the greeting, "Rabbi" (v. 25); and the kiss of the one who dipped with him in the dish. Equally telling is Judas' "Hail, Rabbi", as Pilate's soldiers will "hail" Jesus in their headquarters. Judas has gone over, not merely to the temple leadership but to the world. Judas has chosen money. "Friend," says Jesus, "do what you're here for." No friend of his, and no longer a disciple, but Jesus will not make an enemy even of Judas. He will accept the will of God even in the one who betrays him, and as he is handed over by him into the hands of sinners.

But one of those with Jesus, not described as a disciple, draws a sword, strikes the slave of the high priest and cuts off his ear. This is of deep significance. First, Jesus forbids it, and not only because those who take the sword will perish by the sword. Jesus has forbidden violence, retaliation: "to those who strike you turn the other cheek" (5:39). Violence flouts the law of love (22:37–40). Those who use violence are, like the traitor, no disciples of his. Second, it is the high priest whose servant has been struck, and the servant represents his master, as Jesus represents his. The servant has been mutilated. He is unfit to stand in the temple, and Matthew says nothing about Jesus' healing him. By arresting Jesus, the high priest has signalled his own downfall and that of all he represents—temple, priesthood and sacrifice. All are superseded in the Passover of Jesus, the Messiah. Third, retaliation misses the point. Jesus could have summoned the heavenly host to his defence. Striking others violates God's will. It is, as Jesus said, the shepherd who must be struck (Zechariah 13:7), as God also struck the firstborn of Egypt that first Passover night. So are the scriptures fulfilled, the law and the prophets. God's firstborn is struck, and his blood is shed, for the Passover of the world.

Finally, Jesus turns to those who arrest him. Swords and clubs are superfluous. They could have taken him at any time in the temple. But, again, "The scriptures of the prophets must be fulfilled." But which, and why? The last and greatest of the "Songs of the Servant" (Isaiah 52:13—53:12) sings of the servant who "was wounded for our transgressions, bruised for our iniquities" (53:5), as, in the Greek of its last verse, "his soul was handed over to death" (53:12). In the garden, Jesus said, "My soul is exceeding sorrowful, even to death." As he said at the table, "The Son of Man goes as it is written of him" (26:24): handed over, delivered, betrayed—all the same word in Greek. This is God's will: Jesus' Passion begins with betrayal, by one of his own, by one whom he had chosen, by one at the table. It begins with a kiss, the ultimate act of gentleness. Violence is forbidden because, at Jesus' Passover, there is no "us" and "them". Jesus dies on "our" account as much as on "theirs", whoever "they" may be. "We" are no less guilty than "they". He suffers first at our hands. His Passover is for the forgiveness of all our sins. The shepherd is struck; the sheep are scattered. "All the disciples forsook him and fled."

1 2

Truth and denial

Matthew 26:57–75 *Wednesday in Holy Week*

As the disciples flee, Peter is left with Jesus, but only at a distance. Now the three-fold pattern traced in the garden, of the disciples' failure and of Jesus' obedience, is repeated in Peter's denial and Jesus' obedience. Matthew recounts three stages of a trial before the temple authorities. First, they seek false evidence against Jesus, "so that they might put him to death". No properly constituted court looks for *false* evidence. The authorities have already determined on Jesus' death and seek justification for their policy. Theologically, however, any evidence that would convict Jesus must be false, because no true evidence could secure his conviction. Jesus is innocent, blameless, the lamb without blemish. Equally, false evidence cannot convict Jesus. They find none to warrant his death. Jesus cannot be convicted in a human court. Those who try to do so, on false evidence, are themselves condemned.

Second, however, testimony is given by two witnesses, and therefore validly, that Jesus had said, "I am able to destroy the temple of God and to build it in three days." This is not denied. Jesus did, indeed, foretell the temple's destruction (24:2). But now, Jesus remains silent. He will not deny what is true, and he will not be convicted on human testimony. And the testimony is true. It speaks of the temple of God rebuilt in Jesus himself as he is raised from the dead; not, however, a replacement temple—Matthew is the most Jewish of evangelists—but its fulfilment. Jesus has come to fulfil the law and the prophets (5:17). Jesus, risen, Emmanuel, God-with-us is what the temple was for Israel, our meeting place with God. Jesus, in whose covenant is the forgiveness of sins, is our place of propitiation and atonement. Jesus is the Passover, the sacrifice. He is himself, crucified, the heart and fulfilment of the temple's purpose.

Third, therefore, unable to convict Jesus on either true or false testimony, the high priest invites him to convict himself, on oath, before God. "Tell us if you are the Messiah, the Son of God." "You have said so," says Jesus. Jesus forbade oaths (5:34). He will not answer on oath; to do so would impugn his truth. But he will not deny the truth in the question. Rather, by his "You have said", Jesus shows that the high priest already knows the answer, and is himself condemned by denying what he knows to be true.

Then Jesus testifies, freely, to them all, "From now on, you will see the Son of Man seated at the right hand of Power, and coming on the clouds of heaven" (Psalm 110:1; Daniel 7:13). *From now on* the Son of Man, whom they will destroy, will reign at God's right hand, until he comes in all the majesty of God's self. It is for *this* that Jesus is condemned: not as Messiah: many claimed messiahship and were even supported. Not as Son of God: this could refer to a divine appointment as king, or to a recognizably righteous person. Jesus is condemned because he interprets his sonship of God in terms of reigning with God, as sharing with or *in* God what it is to be God, as the embodiment of God's reign, of his kingdom. Jesus will die for what he is, and for his witness to this truth. Those, however, who worship his God but cannot receive this truth must condemn him for blasphemy.

Where Jesus, however, testifies to the truth and gives himself to death, Peter denies the truth. In the garden, neither Peter nor the others could stay with Jesus, watch and pray with him. Already he is separated from him; now he will disown him. Three times he is challenged, twice by maids of the high priest, those with the least status in his household. The first challenges Peter to his face. The second exposes him to the crowd: he was with Jesus of Nazareth. The third comes from the bystanders themselves: "You're one of them, your accent gives you away." Peter is pushed into three public denials. First, before them all, he says, "I don't know what you're saying". Fatal! Jesus had said, "Whoever denies me before others, I will deny before my Father in heaven" (10:33). Peter has forfeited his salvation. Second, Peter says, with an oath, "I don't know the man." He has renounced his discipleship. Third, he repeats this with another oath (again a contrast with Jesus!), and a curse, and Matthew's Greek implies a curse upon Jesus. Peter's apostasy is complete, and the cock crows.

Is Peter's only a terrible mirror of our own frailty? There is more. Both maids challenge him with being with Jesus of Nazareth. The bystanders challenge him as a member of the group around Jesus, recognizable by his speech, and Matthew tells of a little while between challenges two and three. Here, in miniature, is the persecution of the earliest Church. Opposition is first to those who take the name of Jesus, and it is specifically Jewish. But as the Church grows, and other tongues are added, especially Greek, membership of the Church becomes the issue and opposition comes from other quarters, pagan and imperial. But the fatal step was still to deny Jesus, "I do not know the man!" We know too, from Paul's first letter to Corinth that some in that wider world said, "Let Jesus be cursed!" (1 Corinthians 12:3).

There is, too, a further implication of Peter forfeiting his very salvation by his first, direct, denial. In this Gospel (contrast Mark 16:7), Peter is not specifically included among those to whom the women are to give the message of the resurrection. Is Matthew's final verdict, then, perdition for Peter? No, for he has affirmed Peter's position in the gift of the keys of the kingdom of heaven (16:19), and Peter is, implicitly, among the eleven at their final commissioning (28:16). Rather, it looks as if the church for which Matthew wrote had reservations, at least, concerning his leadership. There is a taste here, perhaps, of politics in the earliest Christian Church. Matthew's deeply Jewish Christian community, still observing the Torah, would recognize James, the Lord's brother, as its head in Jerusalem. It would not so recognize Peter, who had denied his Lord. Many others did, however, as Mark, Luke–Acts and (with some qualification) John testify. Many Gentile churches, no doubt, looked to Paul as their apostle, whose arrest the Jerusalem Church effectively procured (Acts 21:20–28). The history of Christian division goes back a very long way indeed.

As the cock crowed, Peter went out into the night, separated from Jesus, scattered like the rest. He is on his own, self-divorced from the Lord. He wept bitterly. It is not too much to say that he had forfeited his salvation, but that is to neglect the cross and its necessity. Peter must have

Christ die for him, like everyone else. This is the significance of Jesus' washing even Peter's feet (John 13:8–9). Peter, too, must come within the covenant of the forgiveness of sins. Jesus' Passover must include Peter, no less than the rest of us, if he is to be saved.

13

Blood sacrifice

Matthew 27:1–26 *Thursday in Holy Week—Maundy Thursday*

It is now the morning after Passover, and the working out of Jesus' Passover continues. Before Pilate he is silent. He will not deny that he is "king of the Jews"—"You say so." But Jesus is silent against the accusations of the temple leadership, as he was before their council. He is silent before Pilate's encouragement to respond. Jesus cannot be convicted on human testimony, whether false or true. He will die as who he is. This is both his majesty and his meekness, the servant, again, who, "like a lamb that is led to the slaughter, like a sheep that before its shearers is silent, so he did not open his mouth" (Isaiah 53:7). Here is the Passover lamb—blameless.

Consistently, Matthew paints Jesus' innocence. Judas has betrayed "innocent blood"—an innocent life. Pilate knows that the temple leadership has acted out of jealousy. His own wife declares Jesus' innocence. She has had a dream, a divine communication. Even as Pilate sits on the judgement seat, heaven proclaims Jesus' righteousness. Faced with the demand for crucifixion, Pilate asks, "Why, what evil has he done?" A lamb without blemish.

The governor is not unaffected. Holding life and death in his hands, he marvels at a prisoner who offers no defence. And at this point, Matthew subtly changes Mark's story. There is a custom of releasing a prisoner for the people at Passover: to give a man his freedom as they celebrate theirs. Mark's Pilate, reacting to popular clamour, offers to release "The King of the Jews", the title that he gives him, offensive to their ears. Matthew's Pilate offers them a choice: Jesus Bar-abbas or Jesus called Messiah?*

---

* Not all the Greek texts have Barabbas' first name as Jesus.

Pilate comes very close to acknowledging Jesus as what he is. The world's submission to Israel's Messiah is being foreshadowed even as Pilate is driven to crucify him.

But, by exonerating Pilate, Matthew is forcing responsibility for Jesus' death on to the Jewish leadership and people. This is one of the darkest pages in the Gospel. Matthew's Jewish–Christian church emerged out of Judaism in all the bitterness of a split in the family. Perhaps, too, Matthew, like Luke, wanted to show his church to the authorities in a better light than those Jews whose rebellion Rome had, in AD 70, so recently and so violently crushed. The temple leaders bring Jesus to Pilate already resolved on his death. Faced with Pilate's offer, they persuade the people to choose Jesus Bar-abbas and destroy Jesus. The people shout, "Let him be crucified!" And the governor washes his hands (Deuteronomy 21:1–9) for absolution from blood guilt. Pilate will not be responsible: "See to it yourselves", as the priests had said to Judas. "His blood be on us and on our children!" is one of the most terrible verses in all the Gospels, as the Jewish people accept responsibility for the shedding of innocent blood; for the taking of a life declared righteous by Pilate and by God. Matthew wrote these words, and they have sustained Christian anti-Semitism to this day.

What shall we say? First, this is Jesus' Passover. In so far as Jesus dies at the hands of his own people, he dies as the Passover victim, the lamb without blemish. His is the blood of the covenant, innocent, for the forgiveness of sins. In Jewish understanding, the blood is the life. As blood is poured out in sacrifice, so the life is liberated to mediate between the parties to the covenant. In this sacrifice, divine blood is shed for human sin. Jesus gives himself, innocent, unconvicted, for the sins of his people, whether they recognize him or not. This is the measure of divine love.

But the Jews are the people of God. In them, we see ourselves. If their temple is rebuilt in Jesus, we belong with them, and it is we who say, "His blood be on us and on our children!" So we recognize in ourselves the words and deeds which crucified Jesus. Have we desired anyone's death, or rejoiced at anyone's fall? Have we, like Pilate, put expediency or convenience before justice and truth? Have we, as Christians, acknowledged any authority above Jesus, and so betrayed him? Have we walked away when we should have stood up for him and for those who are his? Have we refused to recognize Christ in others—too uncomfortable—and so denied him? If we have, then indeed, "His blood be on us and on our children!"—the blood of the covenant for the forgiveness of sins; the blood of the Passover over ourselves and our families; the blood of the Lamb of God who takes away the sin of the world (John 1:29). Then, truly, this is our Passover, as he gives us the bread of his body and the cup of his blood . . . and washes our feet.

1 4

The Passover of the world

Matthew 27:27–54 *Good Friday*

Handed over for crucifixion by Pilate, Jesus is taken inside the governor's headquarters and subjected to a barrack room entertainment. The whole garrison is gathered against him—600 men. They represent Rome: her power, her empire, even her law. Like the temple leadership before them, they subject Jesus to a humiliation of stripping, spitting and beating. In their case, however, this is bitter, anti-Jewish mockery: fastening one of their scarlet cloaks over Jesus' naked body; putting a mere reed in his right hand (the reed was the symbol on Herod's coins); paying homage to "the King of the Jews". The representative of a people despised by the nations bears the scorn of the nations. And it is they who crown him—with thorns. Two days earlier a woman of his own people had anointed him as king in burial. Now he is crowned by the servants of imperial power, in pain and insult as "King of the Jews". Degradation, insult and bitterness are heaped upon Jesus, the victim of the world's empire and its violence. He bears our iniquities (Isaiah 53:11). He reigns—Messiah, Christ, Anointed One—in suffering. This is the Passover of the world.

Into the fabric of Jesus' humiliation is woven the thread of the scriptures. They give him wine mingled with gall—Psalm 69:21. They cast lots for his clothing—Psalm 22:18. His enemies throw back at him his trust in God—Psalm 22:8. The thread of the scriptures show that this is God's will for him. It is "according to the scriptures" that Roman soldiers crucify Israel's Messiah, under the placard that proclaims him, "This is Jesus, the King of the Jews." A Jew declared to be innocent is crucified between two bandits, outlaws from Israel, criminals to Rome. Rejected on all sides, Jesus bears the *sin* of the world.

Then comes the mockery, the scorn of the people of God for their king. Jesus bears the rejection of God by those who believe themselves his, leaders and people alike. Jesus is derided as Saviour, mocked as king, taunted as Son of God. The tempter comes back: "If you are the Son of God . . . " (4:3,6). The sins of his people are cast upon Jesus, Jesus whose name is above his head, Jesus who "will save his people from their sins" (1:21). But in their mockery, they proclaim him. He will destroy the temple and build it in three days. They attest his saving work. He is the king of Israel. He is "I AM—the Son of God". Jesus, Messiah, reigns in our rejection of him. King of Israel, Christ, Son of God, crucified by Gentiles, mocked by his own, Jesus is the sovereign and Saviour of the world because he bears the sin of the world.

After three hours of darkness, at the ninth hour of the day, Jesus cries, "My God, my God, why have you forsaken me?" He cries as a Son, forsaken by his Father. He cries in Hebrew, in the language and words of scripture. Jesus' God-forsakenness is God's will. As he gives himself, so God has given him. This is the terrible sacrifice, the paradox of Passover, of innocent life given for the guilty. Righteous, blameless, Jesus is God-forsaken because he is bearing the sin of the world. And, in this, Jesus is identifying with every human being in innocent and undeserved suffering—not least with the immense tide of suffering brought about precisely by the systemic injustice and sin of the world. "My God, why? What I have I done?" Nothing to deserve this. But this is how life is, and in Jesus God has associated himself with it. This is the Passover of all humanity.

"And the curtain of the Temple was torn in two from top to bottom." The holy place is broken open. God has deserted his temple and hangs here in the body of his Son. Jesus has destroyed the temple and will rebuild it in three days. As he breathes his last, Jesus has broken, and broken through the old order of sin and death. This is why Matthew tells of an earthquake, rocks split, graves opened and the raising of Israel's saints. Jesus' crucifixion is of cosmic significance. In it is anticipated the end, when the dead will be raised and this order will pass away. The centurion and his soldiers recognize Jesus as Son of God, the first of the Gentiles to do so. Creation is delivered from slavery. This is the Passover of the world.

15

Raised from the dead

Matthew 28:1–10 (Acts 10:34–43; Colossians 3:1–4)   *Easter Day*

How different Matthew's story is! From Mark, we should have heard of three women coming to Jesus' tomb to anoint his body, finding the stone already moved away, and a young man in white inside. He gives them a message for the disciples, but they flee, terrified, and tell no one.

Matthew tells of the two "Marys" coming to see a tomb guarded by soldiers. No mention of anointing! That was done five days ago by a woman at Bethany. They witness an earthquake, and the stone's removal by an angel. The angel gives them, however, the same message. They run to deliver it and meet Jesus. The stories are different: the message is the same.

That Jesus' tomb was empty is not recorded outside the Gospels. St Paul, our earliest Christian writer, never mentions it, nor is it included in any of the other Epistles. It is not mentioned in any of Peter's sermons in the Acts. In an age of grave-robbers, stories of an empty tomb would convince nobody.

The earliest Christian tradition was of Jesus' appearing. That was the tradition that Paul received, and how he encountered the Lord. We hear typical Christian preaching of the resurrection in the Acts: "They put him to death by hanging him on a tree but God raised him up and gave him to appear, not to all the people, but to us who were chosen by God as witnesses ... " (Acts 10:39–41). Both Acts and Paul mention Jesus' burial, to confirm the reality of his death. It was the gospel of the risen Christ which the apostles first took to the world.

The tradition of the empty tomb came later. Luke's account includes features from both Matthew and Mark. John's story is different again, but he also tells of Mary Magdalene alone at the tomb. Why do the accounts differ? Because the evangelists saw different significance in the empty tomb for the life and faith of their people. The Gospels were written less to convert outsiders than to nourish the faith of the churches. Their various accounts, composed under the direction of the Holy Spirit, were written to help us understand the resurrection: how we may speak, truthfully, of Jesus risen from the dead.

Mark's account of the empty tomb is of a profound mystery. Matthew, however, has already told us that Jesus' tomb was sealed and a guard placed over it on the day of his burial, lest his body be removed for a counterfeit resurrection. Why, then, the earthquake, and the angel, in the presence of the two women? Matthew tells of earthquakes: they are signs of God at work. He tells of an "earthquake" of the sea, when Jesus calms the storm (8:24) and of all Jerusalem "shaken" when Jesus enters as king (21:10). He tells of an earthquake as Jesus dies, the rocks split, the tombs opened, the bodies of Israel's saints raised—the final achievement of Jesus' Passover, the resurrection of the dead. So, at Jesus' tomb, in this earthquake, God's work is done.

An angel, too, signifies God at work. He is clothed with divine majesty. He acts, he interprets, he delivers a message. The earthquake, like that when Israel's saints are raised, is the moment of Jesus' resurrection: God's breaking him from the bonds of death. The angel opens the tomb, *and he doesn't come out.* There is nothing to see, only, as the angel says, "the place where he lay". Jesus "is not here, for he has been raised". This is the resurrection.

The angel declares the gospel: "He has been raised from the dead", and sends the women to the disciples with the message. Running with it joyfully, they meet Jesus, who confirms it: "Tell my brothers to go to Galilee, there they will see me." Galilee, Galilee of the Gentiles (4:15), the place of their calling, and now of their commissioning as apostles (meaning "those who are sent") to the world (28:16–20). In other words, to see Jesus, as the women did, you must obey him; be obedient, as he was, to death, because he has been raised and will raise those who belong to him.

And this: Jesus greets the women with the same word as Judas used with his kiss, and the soldiers used in their humiliation of him, "Hail!"

The word with which Jesus was handed over to death, with which he was crowned and proclaimed as king by the representatives of the Roman Empire, is now used by Jesus to greet those who were faithful, who witnessed his cross. Jesus has triumphed. He reigns. His is a global greeting. Those who follow him faithfully will see him.

The Church was made by the gospel of Christ crucified and risen. It was sustained by the experience of Christ in the community of the Church and in lives transformed. People found themselves in Christ, united to him, corporately and individually. They found Christ in each other, in service, forgiveness, encouragement and correction. They found Christ in themselves, indwelling, empowering, healing, transforming. They found Christ in their midst, especially when they gathered, as he had commanded, to proclaim his death, to re-enact his sacrifice, to celebrate his Passover. Christ was risen, and they knew it.

On the occasion for which this sermon was written, it concluded with the following two paragraphs:

On Good Friday evening, in the Gospel of John, we proclaimed the cross. As, in the last hymn, thirty of you sang your praise of Christ crucified, I saw the people of God, Christ in you. On another Good Friday evening, some years ago, as you left the church I exclaimed, "Look at those lovely Christian faces!" You are different, you are changed, you shine with the presence of Christ, because you didn't spend the evening "in", or at bingo or shopping. You came to renew your identity in Christ, as you have done this morning, and as you will do when you receive the bread of his body and the cup of his blood.

One face that other Good Friday belonged to a soldier, a working man, a husband and father: a Christian man, regular in church, faithful in service to this parish. Within months he was dead. But if Christ shone in him then, he reigns with Christ now. After a week in which we have buried two more of our members, this is our hope. As long as there are people whose faces shine with the grace of Christ, the peace of Christ, the love of Christ and the truth of Christ, his Church will live.

The Passion according to Luke

Sidelights on the Cross

Introduction

In his account of Jesus' Passion, Matthew closely follows Mark, editing or adding to the story. In Luke's account, the differences are greater, through the omission of some incidents, re-ordering of events and additions. The latter include some "last words" of Jesus at the supper, an interview of Jesus with Herod, a lament by Jesus over Jerusalem as he is taken for crucifixion, and a dialogue between Jesus and those crucified with him. Some of the more significant of Luke's alterations are explored here.

A Gentile himself, Luke seems to have been writing for a Greek-speaking, predominantly Gentile church. He was, however, clearly familiar with the Hebrew scriptures in their Greek translation. He shows Jesus proclaiming the imminence of the kingdom of God in his deeds and in his teaching, and his death as bringing it about. His writing stresses the reality of the events he describes, for example, in the descent of the Holy Spirit upon Jesus at his baptism "in bodily form" as a dove (3:22). Jesus' Passion and resurrection are the "hinge" between the two volumes of his work, the Gospel and the Acts of the Apostles, so that the mission of Jesus and his disciples in Galilee is continued as the mission of Jesus in his Church to the nations of the Roman Empire, culminating with Paul's arrival in Rome itself. A particular theme running through both the Gospel and the Acts is that of repentance and the forgiveness of sins (e.g. Luke 5:32; 13:3,5; 19:1–10; 24:47; Acts 2:38; 3:26; 5:31; etc.). Unsurprisingly, this is carried through into Luke's presentation of Jesus' Passion, and of his resurrection.

16

A last meal together

Luke 22:1–23　　　　　　　　　　*Monday in Holy Week*

We will never know quite how Jesus died, exactly what happened in his last hours. We know only that, since that night, meal and cross, cross and meal, have been inextricably connected. Factual certainty is unattainable because we cannot go back behind the evangelists, who differ. But they, drawing on eyewitnesses and tradition, are the privileged witnesses to Jesus, his life, death and resurrection. By attending to the evangelists, we attend to the Word, to the Gospel. By attending to the individual evangelists, we attend to their particular insights into the significance of Jesus' death. We cannot get closer than this.

At the beginning of Luke's account of the Passion, two things stand out. First, Luke says nothing of an anointing of Jesus at Bethany, common to the other Gospels. Without that anointing, Judas' conspiracy to betray Jesus (and it is Judas who initiates it) seems immediately to precede the supper. Then Luke includes Jesus' prediction of his betrayal not at the beginning but at the end of the supper. So Luke surrounds the supper with talk of betrayal, the betrayal which we remember every time we celebrate the supper. By attending to this, we shall see how Luke understands what Jesus did on the cross.

For—and this is the second thing that stands out—when Luke wrote his Gospel, he almost certainly omitted the words referring to the bread of Jesus' body as "given for you", the command to do this in remembrance of him, and the cup after supper as "the covenant in my blood". These things were added later, to harmonize Luke's account with the other Gospels and Paul. Luke himself gave a different account of the supper, as we shall see. Luke, the Gentile, did not understand the cross in the

Jewish terms of blood sacrifice, as Matthew and Paul did. For Luke, then, the supper is not the institution of a memorial of Jesus' sacrifice. Rather, it is the institution of the fellowship meal of the new community which, throughout the Acts, Luke calls, "the breaking of bread". This is the common meal of those who recognize, in Jesus' death and resurrection, the universal in-breaking of the kingdom of God.

Therefore, when Luke begins his account of the conspiracy to kill Jesus, he refers to "the festival of Unleavened Bread which is called the Passover". Commentators may suggest that Luke was mistaken: the Days of Unleavened Bread begin with and follow Passover. But Luke, by privileging "Unleavened Bread" over Passover, is making a point. In Exodus, Unleavened Bread, more so even than Passover, is specifically connected with Israel's "coming out" of Egypt (Exodus 12:14-20,33-34,39). In his account of the transfiguration, Luke has Jesus discuss with Moses his "exodus" which he was to accomplish at Jerusalem (9:31). For Luke, then, the cross is the way in which Jesus wins freedom for his people, a freedom which Luke will connect specifically with repentance and the forgiveness of sins.

The chief priests and scribes already want Jesus dead, "for", says Luke, "they feared the people". Is Luke casting them, perhaps, in the role of Pharaoh, the oppressor? At all events, they welcome Judas' approach. But why did he do it? Luke no more records his motive than any of the evangelists. He says, simply, that Satan entered him. Satan, for Luke, is the ruler of demonic powers, whom Jesus saw fall from heaven as the demons submitted to his emissaries (10:18); whom Jesus equates with Beelzebul, the prince of demons (11:18), who had bound a crippled woman, a "daughter of Abraham" (13:16). Satan, then, takes possession of Judas. Judas acts as a man possessed and, so possessed, joins forces with the temple leadership and their officials, accepting their money. There is nothing to suggest that Judas knew that he was possessed or showed evidence of possession. Quite the contrary, it was a mystery to his brothers at the supper who could possibly do this. Evil seldom advertises itself. It is enough that Judas exchanges the kingdom of God for the opposition, the powers of this world and their currency. This should give pause to us all.

It is worth noticing too that Luke says of Judas, rather formally, that he was called "Iscariot". This, too, puzzles the scholars. Did he come from Kerioth in southern Judea? Or was he one of the "Sicarii", associated with the Zealots, known for their *sicae*, or daggers? We shall see.

The Day of Unleavened Bread arrives. Again, like Mark before him (Mark 14:12), Luke's timing is inaccurate. The Passover lambs were slaughtered on the day before the feast which, by Jewish reckoning, began at sunset. But if Luke, a Greek writing for Greeks, is reckoning by Greek time, the lambs are slaughtered in the afternoon for consumption later that evening. Again, in stressing the connection of Passover with unleavened bread, Luke highlights its connotations of freedom. Jesus takes the initiative and sends two of his foremost disciples into Jerusalem to prepare the Passover. However we understand those mysterious arrangements, involving a man carrying a water jar, they lead to preparations focused on a large room upstairs. No more than any other evangelist does Luke mention anyone going to the temple to slaughter a lamb. Either we take this for granted, or it is of great significance.

The meal begins, solemnly: Jesus and his disciples reclining; the Passover which Jesus, having eagerly desired to eat it with his disciples, now explicitly does not eat. He will not do so, he says, until the kingdom of God is fulfilled. This Passover, this festival of freedom, so eagerly awaited by Jesus, denotes the imminence of the kingdom but not yet its arrival. For that, Jesus must suffer. The meal is a gift-in-advance of the kingdom, in which Jesus will eat with his own.

Then, in Luke's account of the supper, the order of bread and cup is reversed. First, Jesus gives the cup, telling his friends to divide it among themselves. He will no more drink the fruit of the vine than he will eat the Passover until the kingdom of God comes. The cup conveys the gladness of the kingdom, but the kingdom comes only through Jesus' death. This is the "cup" that he must drink. This order, of cup followed by bread, has a parallel in St Paul: "The cup of blessing which we bless ... The bread which we break ..." (1 Corinthians 10:16). Paul interpreted it differently, but his order is the same as Luke's. Only now, having declined the cup of wine, does Jesus do what was done at every Passover with the bread: take it, give thanks, break it and give. "This," says Jesus simply, "is my body."

This is me. In giving his disciples the bread, which is himself, Jesus is giving them the kingdom, which will come in his death.

Then, in the closest possible relation to the bread broken and given, Jesus says, "But see, the hand of him who betrays me is with me at the table": the hand of Judas, the *sicarios,* the hand with the dagger. On the day when the Passover must be sacrificed, Judas will wield the knife. Meal and cross, cross and meal are inextricably linked. Jesus is himself his Passover. This Passover he cannot eat. He is—as John says—the Lamb (John 1:29). He goes, as has been determined, to his divinely appointed destiny, fulfilling the pattern of Israel's history, first written in her deliverance from Egypt. His death wins freedom for God's people. Not that Judas is relieved of responsibility: "Woe to the man by whom he is betrayed." Judas represents us in our refusal of the kingdom, our choice of other loyalties, our turning against the Son of Man.

17

Famous last words

Luke 2:24-38   *Tuesday in Holy Week*

In Luke's Gospel, distinctively, as Jesus presides at the supper, he is himself the Passover, giving himself for his own, giving himself to bring in the kingdom. As Luke's account differs from Mark and Matthew, the differences continue as the story moves on. Because Matthew's account stands first in the Gospels, and is based upon Mark's, we may be inclined to accept it as normative—a tendency reinforced, for some, by J. S. Bach's sublime interpretation of it. But Luke is an evangelist in his own right. He wrote a two-volume work, Gospel and Acts, for a church in the Gentile world. He tells the story for his community. He says nothing of the disciples deserting Jesus. Instead, Jesus assures his apostles (those whom he sends, for so he introduces them as the supper begins, (22:14)) of their place in his kingdom. Before that there is teaching on greatness, which Mark and Matthew place elsewhere. Afterwards comes Jesus' prediction of Peter's failure, but in terms which specifically commission him as leader. This is followed by a strange passage about apostles carrying swords.

All rather difficult! But Jesus' teaching on greatness is followed by his assuring the apostles of their greatness, as those who have proved faithful. The same teaching on greatness is reflected in the terrible humbling of Peter, and in how Jesus instructs him to lead the apostles. The strange incident of the swords will humble the whole twelve. Luke is telling us Jesus' last words, to his apostles and to his Church, Luke's Church and ours.

Around the supper table, then, just after Jesus has foretold his betrayal, the question arises of who seems to be the greatest? If betrayal means going over to the other side, self-seeking is closely related to it. It means exploiting our Christian faith and identity for our own benefit. It denies Jesus as *our* Lord, and our obligation to Christian service. Jesus begins with kingship as exercised in the ancient world, as absolute power, but at its best, benevolent despotism. Authoritarian power was expected to be used for the common good. Jesus, however, turns this on its head, to argue, not for democracy, but for personal service. The Church is to model God's kingdom, not mimic political systems. To a church where leadership was by elders, whom the younger serve, Jesus insists that roles be reversed. The eldest must be as the youngest, the leader as one who serves. He himself is among them as a waiter, even as he presides. He is, again, their Passover, giving himself for them to supply their every need. This is Jesus' model for Christian leadership, not authority, privilege, position or power. Clergy no longer receive the deference of yesteryear!

Then, instead of foretelling their desertion, Jesus assures the apostles of their place in his kingdom. This is a radical departure from Mark and Matthew. Certainly, their eating and drinking at the Passover table is a foretaste of their feasting with Jesus in the kingdom to come. Certainly, too, their calling as apostles and their place in God's kingdom is by Jesus' appointment or gift. But Jesus' disciples are nowhere recorded as standing by him in his testing or trials. And what does he mean by their judging the twelve tribes of Israel? The answer lies in the longer story that Luke tells, through the Acts of the Apostles. Israel continued predominantly to refuse Jesus as her Messiah and the apostles' preaching of him. When Jerusalem was destroyed in AD 70, the Jewish church went with it. The future of the Christian faith lay with the Gentile mission spearheaded by Paul, with which the last half, and more, of the Acts is concerned. What was then the position of the twelve, who had suffered trials and rejection, and whose witness seemed a failure? An honoured place in the kingdom, at the top table with Jesus, and with divine authority over those who had rejected them! Jesus is faithful to his own, and will be to any church whose witness, if faithful, goes unheeded or is rejected.

Next, Jesus addresses their leader in person urgently: "Simon, Simon"—not Peter—already his failure is in view. They will all be sifted like wheat, shaken together as in a sieve, tested by Satan. Their mission will be perilous. But Jesus has already prayed that Simon's faith may not fail completely. So Jesus predicts Peter's apostasy. Denying his Lord three times means that Peter is renouncing his apostleship: a total failure. By this, he will become the least of them. Turned again, however—converted—he is to strengthen the faith of the others with, perhaps, the particular faith of the convert. Together with the command to serve, it is a wonderful definition of Christian leadership—of episcopal leadership, of pastoral leadership, of papal leadership: to support, affirm, encourage, strengthen and develop what is in others; not to lord it, but to build the people of God.

Finally, Jesus alerts the apostles to their changed situation. When he had first sent them out (9:1-6), without purse, bag or sandals, they had (paradoxically!) been accepted as their king's emissaries by a welcoming people. Now the king is rejected. Henceforth they will need their own resources. "But now, he who has a purse must take it, and likewise a bag, and he who has none must sell his cloak and buy a sword" (22:36). At the very least, the Christian gospel is going to be proclaimed in conditions of enmity.

But this is for the future. As Jesus and the twelve go out from the supper, the possession of swords marks them as outlaws, transgressors. Two swords between them are enough to implicate them all. Jesus will be arrested in their company. Isaiah is fulfilled: "And he was reckoned with the transgressors" (Isaiah 53:12). The transgressors are not those with whom Jesus will be crucified. The transgressors are his own. One of them would use his sword and suffer Jesus' rebuke (22:50-51). So Jesus will die for his own. And with the apostles in transgression stand we ourselves. As we are part of this world's violence, we too are guilty. But as Jesus dies, the centurion-in-charge, a man trained for violence, pronounces him righteous. The righteous dies for the transgressors, the innocent for the guilty. This is the heart of the message of the cross.

1 8

Ultimate failure

Luke 22:54–71 *Wednesday in Holy Week*

With Jesus now arrested and brought to the high priest's house, Luke's account of his Passion continues, with Peter's denial of him and of Jesus' own appearance before Israel's leaders. The two are set in deliberate contrast: where Peter cannot testify to his Lord, Jesus testifies to Israel, represented by her highest civil and religious authority.

The scene is the high priest's residence. Somewhere, visible from the central courtyard or hall, Jesus is in custody, undergoing verbal and physical abuse: a sadistic "blind man's buff"—"Prophesy—who hit you!"— hooding and deprivation of sleep. But in the middle of the courtyard a fire is lit. Around it sit those who arrested Jesus. In the middle of them sits Peter, suddenly alone and surrounded. If he is recognized, he becomes the centre of hostile attention. This is a situation almost guaranteed to bring out the child in anyone—alone, frightened and vulnerable in a hostile world. Adulthood, confidence and self-assurance are stripped away. Peter is lost—the lost sheep without his Lord. And what has happened to the others?

Let us notice, then, the exchanges between Peter and those who seek to expose him. Maid: "This man also was with him." Peter: "I don't know him." Man: "You also are one of them." Peter: "I am not." Second man, emphatically: "Certainly this man also was with him, for he is a Galilean." Peter: "I don't know what you're talking about." Notice the "also", three times. So Peter is led to deny all association with Jesus, first with Jesus himself. He does not know him. He is not a disciple. This is the root of apostasy. Second, he denies belonging with the others, the twelve. He denies his apostleship, as one of those sent out by Jesus, entrusted with his commission. Third, he even denies himself, his own person and roots, as a Galilean. Peter denies everything that he is. Spiritually, socially and personally, he is cast adrift.

But it is not the end for Peter. Certainly, Jesus' prediction is fulfilled as the cock crows. Jesus looks at Peter ... But Peter remembers, says Luke, "the word of the Lord"—a word of divine insight and power. By foretelling his disaster, Jesus has set the scene for Peter's rescue. Even his apostasy is within God's purpose. Jesus has prayed that his faith may not fail, has set in motion God's rescue of a loyal and faithful servant. Already he has appointed him to a future role as leader—strengthening his brothers (22:32)—when he has turned around, come to himself and recovered his identity in the risen Lord.

Here is the honesty of the Gospel. Why not leave out the story of Peter? It is only an incident on the way to Jesus' death. All four tell it, however. The Gospel would not be the Gospel without the story of Peter. He was the first chosen by Jesus, the leader of the disciples, the first to recognize him as Messiah, the first leader of the infant church and, by the Holy Spirit's direction, the first to preach to Gentiles. Trying hardest, he fell furthest. It was as restored by Jesus that Peter achieved what he did. Weakness and failure are recognized in those whom Jesus chooses. Nothing is beyond the scope of his death, forgiveness and love. He chooses us as we are and makes of us what we will allow him to make. Whatever we may do for him requires first our conversion to him, so that whatever he achieves in us is by his Spirit, his presence and his love.

Contrast the scene next morning in the council chamber: Jesus arraigned before the representatives of Israel after a night's abuse. Like Peter's examiners, they demand an open declaration of who he is: "If you're the Messiah, tell us!" Jesus refuses to answer in their terms: "If I tell you, you will never believe (the Greek is emphatic); and if I question you, you will never answer." There is in his accusers a settled opposition, incapable of accepting him, of listening, and of entering into the dialogue that alone makes acceptance possible. So is human sin expressed, a radical, even wilful, blindness and deafness to God, present in all of us, and the more marked the greater the interests and position that we seek to defend.

But Jesus gives an answer, in his own terms, in words derived from scripture: "But from now on the Son of Man will be seated at the right hand of the power of God" (Psalm 110:1). This is an assertion of supreme and eternal sovereignty, and it provokes a further question from them all, "Are you, then, the Son of God?" This Jesus will not deny. "You say that I am" is an acknowledgment of their recognition, even in their refusal of him. Had not Peter's first recognition of him as Messiah (9:20) been provoked by Jesus' question, "But who do you say that I am?" "I am" too, in this context, carries a suggestion of the divine name (Exodus 3:14). Jesus bears his testimony where Peter could not. Israel's leaders confess him, paradoxically, as they examine him. They accept his testimony even as they condemn him. Jesus will be crucified, for Israel, as what he is, the Messiah, the Son of Man and Son of God.

1 9

Unexpected friends

Luke 23:6–12   *Maundy Thursday*

On the evening of Maundy Thursday, we re-enact, with bread and wine, the Passover of Jesus, in all its significance as it conveys to us the benefits of his saving death. In following Luke's Gospel of the Passion, we have reached the point at which Jesus is handed over to be crucified. And again, Luke puts a different slant on the story. He invites us to see something different from what we are used to. Only Luke tells of Pilate's sending Jesus to Herod. Scholars question it as history. Why, then, did Luke include it in his Gospel, his account of the good news of Jesus? What is it about Jesus' death that he wanted to convey in this episode?

Luke begins with the leaders of Israel bringing Jesus before Pilate, determined on his death. As in no other Gospel, they lay specific charges against him, all with political overtones: "seducing the nation" from loyalty to the empire; "forbidding tribute to Caesar"—denying him his taxes; "making himself out to be Christ, a king"—a pretender, a rival to Pilate and the emperor. So Pilate asks, with studied contempt, "You, are you the king of the Jews?" "You say so," replies Jesus. He will not deny it. He will not claim it, but he will accept it as true, even if uttered in contempt. Pilate dismisses the charges as unfounded, but when they are repeated, and Galilee mentioned, he sends Jesus to Herod.

Herod, or Herod Antipas, a son of Herod the Great, was Rome's puppet, the client king who ruled Galilee in the north. Southern Israel, under Pilate, was directly under Roman rule. Herod had murdered John the Baptist, who had criticized his marriage to Herodias, both his own niece and the wife of his half-brother, also called Herod. Jesus had been warned (13:31) that Herod wanted to murder him too. But Herod had wanted to see him, ever since people started suggesting that this wonderworker was John the Baptist raised from the dead.

What Luke tells us about Jesus before Herod is very like what Mark and Matthew tell us about Jesus before Pilate. Herod questions him. Jesus is silent. Israel's leaders press vehement but unspecific charges against him. Then the mocking, which Mark attributes to Pilate's soldiers, is done by Herod and his. What is Luke showing us in this? We must, again, go back to Mark. Mark tells of a purple cloak and a crown of thorns: Jesus treated with a vicious parody of the homage due by his troops to a Roman emperor. Mark invites us to see Jesus proclaimed as sovereign even by those who abuse him.

So here are Herod and his soldiers. Luke uses a grand word, suggesting a parade. They clothe Jesus in a bright, splendid, shining robe. They, too, treat him with contempt, but in a parody of the homage due to a king of Israel. Jesus is invested as king of Israel—the real thing—by Herod and his army. As king of Israel, he will die. Israel is implicated in his death, from Herod downwards. Just as Jesus dies for his disciples, implicated as outlaws, so he dies for the nation too.

There is, however, a "shadow side" to Luke's account at this point. Luke has written an elegant account of the Gospel, in good Greek, addressed to "Theophilus", a "lover of God", for the wider society of the Roman Empire. To the extent that Luke emphasizes the responsibility of Israel, and especially its leadership, for Jesus' death, he lessens that of Pilate and the empire that he represents. After Jesus' resurrection, the call to repentance will be addressed to the citizens of that empire (e.g. to the citizens of Athens, Acts 17:30–31, and finally to the citizens of Rome, as Paul travels there), but it will be addressed first to the Jewish people (Acts 2:38; 3:19; 4:10; 5:31). Thus, in the attribution of responsibility for Jesus' death, and in the repeated portrayal of the Jewish refusal of the gospel, was planted one of the roots of Christian anti-Semitism. If we, who read or hear the gospel from a standpoint of faith, are not to perpetuate the terrible history that ensued, we must hear the call to repentance addressed to Israel as addressed to us, who are incorporated into God's people by Jesus' death (Romans 11:17–18). Repentance, the recognition of our enduring complicity with the "sin of the world", is both the necessary antidote to self-righteousness and the key to a living faith.

Herod sends Jesus back to Pilate robed, as a king. Pilate again maintains Jesus' innocence until, shouted down by Israel's leaders in Jerusalem, he hands him over to their will. (Again, Luke's attribution of responsibility is consistent.) But "on that day Herod and Pilate became friends with each other; before this there had been enmity between them". Herod and Pilate: both implicated in the cross. Both condemned, by abuse or sentence, a man they knew to be innocent. Are they simply partners in crime? Is it simply a case of "my enemy's enemy is my friend"? Rather, on the day that Jesus dies, they are reconciled: Jew and Gentile, Jewish puppet and imperial overlord; the representatives of a subject people and of a global empire. The "dividing wall of hostility" (Ephesians 2:14) is broken down as Jesus dies for all.

Here, then, is Luke's Gospel for a divided world: for societies divided by race, wealth, aspiration and identity (and, not least, for the Holy Land, divided by walls and settlements); for nations facing off against one another across contested boundaries or with competing interests and ideologies; for a world in which disagreement and division threatens our ability to address the transnational catastrophe of accelerating climate change, environmental collapse and species loss. This is also Luke's Gospel for churches divided from one another, and for communions and churches divided within themselves. Herod and Pilate, both in their sins, guilty of Jesus' death, are reconciled by his cross. The Gospel becomes fruitful as we recognize our part in the all-too-human fears and rivalries that led to Jesus' rejection and death. So may we also begin to recognize our part in the conflicts in which, actively or passively, we are involved; in the processes which have brought us to where we are. Then we may begin to be able to recognize the "other" not simply as the enemy to whom we are opposed, in whom we see only a threat, but potentially as our friend in a new and different future.

2 0

The salvation of the world

Luke 23:26–49   *Good Friday*

At the cross, Luke's story reaches its climax. No other Gospel tells of Jesus' warning of impending judgement on Jerusalem as he is led out of the city. No other Gospel records his forgiveness of those who crucify him. Only Luke includes the detail that one of those crucified with Jesus turned to him. Here, finally, for Luke is the significance of the cross.

Salvation and judgement are the two sides of the same coin, the alternative consequences of our choice in relation to God. Jesus has been declared innocent of evil, as Pilate asked (23:22), "Why, what evil has he done?" But he has been exchanged for Barabbas, convicted of murder. He has been handed over for crucifixion as an evildoer. Two other evildoers, says Luke, were led away to death with him, and that, literally, makes Jesus an evildoer with them. As Paul says (2 Corinthians 5:21) God "made him to be sin who knew no sin". But if you exchange good for evil, judgement must follow—hence Jesus' final words of warning to Jerusalem.

But then, as Jesus is crucified, unexpected words break the flow of the story: "Father, forgive them; they don't know what they're doing" v. 34).* In our law, ignorance is no defence. But here is sovereign grace, breaking in where our law would condemn. Here forgiveness is sought for those who are engaged in the unspeakable; forgiveness preceding the least glimmer of repentance, forgiveness for those in the midst of their sins, who crucify the Son of God.

---

*   Indeed, the sharpness of the break and the evidence of the manuscript sources suggest that these words may not have been in Luke's original text, but may have been added to it, although at a very early date.

For whom is Jesus praying? The soldiers at their work? Luke means more than this. He has not mentioned soldiers since the mockery of Herod's troops. Pilate handed Jesus over to the will of the people of Jerusalem, their leaders first. It is they, as we have seen, whom Luke holds responsible for crucifying Jesus. He returns to the theme in the early chapters of the Acts. Jesus' forgiveness, then, is his forgiveness of all who crucify him—of priests and leaders, of people, of Pilate, Herod, and the soldiers too. This, too, is forgotten in the dreadful tradition of anti-Semitism. For who is it who prays but the King of Israel, Messiah, the Christ of God, inseparable in will and deed from the Father, whose prayer accomplishes what it wills? Those who crucify him are forgiven. After his resurrection, the gospel of repentance and forgiveness of sins will be preached to Jerusalem and to the world (24:47; Acts 1:8; 2:38–39). God's forgiveness in Christ is the ground of our repentance, not a response to it. God's forgiveness is certain. This is the grace of the gospel.

So we turn to the criminals, the evildoers, with whom Jesus is crucified. If Jesus' word of forgiveness was universal, this encounter could not be more personal, as both judgement and salvation are. Hanging as they do, the three of them are accursed under the Law of Israel, excluded from God's presence, consigned to destruction. This Jesus faces with them. One of them joins in the mockery: "Aren't you the Messiah? Save yourself and us!" All the mockery is about saving and messiahship—Messiah doing what he is supposed to do, but "saving" in its basest form, a travesty of his mission, saving himself—significantly, in Luke's account, the third and last temptation (4:9–11).

The other, however, says, "Do you not fear God, since you are under the same condemnation? And we indeed justly, for we are receiving what our deeds deserve. But this man has done nothing wrong." This is a voice that recognizes the imminence of personal judgement, that accepts responsibility for his deeds and recognizes Jesus' innocence—the first Jew to do so. Now the exchange of the righteous for the evildoer can bear fruit. As the righteous man dies the death of the evildoer, so he can acquit the evildoer through death. Our sins become his. The curse is lifted and we are set free.

"Jesus, remember me when you come into your kingdom." Instead of barracking the Messiah, this man pleads the saving name: "Jesus".

Nothing more is necessary. This is the name for the forgiveness of sins, the name by which we must be saved (Acts 4:12). "Jesus, remember me." Do as God does in faithfulness to his covenant, when his people turn to him for rescue, confessing their sins. Remember me, when you enter into that sovereign power which is yours and his.

"Today, you will be with me in Paradise." The last word. Jesus' cross has done its work. The first of those who turn to him has been saved, delivered from the curse, released from condemnation, restored to the presence of God. Paradise is the realm of heaven, but it carries with it the memory of that first garden, Eden, where grew the tree of life, from which humanity is banished for its disobedience. To be in Paradise is to be restored to what we were created to be, in freedom with one another without pressure, guilt or shame, in the perfect communion of love which is the embrace of Jesus Christ.

2 1

Lord both of the dead and of the living

Acts 10:34-43; 1 Corinthians 15:19-26; Luke 24:1-12　　　Easter Day

> For to this end Christ died and lived again, that he might be Lord both of the dead and of the living.
>
> *Romans 14:9*

At early dawn, a group of women stood at an empty tomb where the body of Jesus should have been. There was no mistake. They had seen him buried and how his body was laid. Suddenly, two men are beside them in dazzling white. Where did they come from? Mark tells of a young man dressed in white; Matthew of an angel who rolled back the stone and sat on it. The key to the differences is that each evangelist tells of the resurrection in order to bring out some particular aspect of its significance. Where, then, did Luke's two figures come from—dressed as angels, who speak as one, who declare a divine secret, the gospel of the Resurrection?

In Genesis, two angels come to Sodom, to execute God's judgement against it and to save Abraham's nephew, Lot. They, too, speak and act as one. Before dawn on the day of Sodom's destruction they rescue Lot and his family. They are God's angels of salvation and judgement—salvation for those who follow God's ways, judgement for those who do not. In Luke's Gospel, uniquely, Jesus quotes the judgement on Sodom in the days of Lot as a foretaste of the judgement on the "day of the Son of Man" (Luke 17:27-30). These two at the tomb, then, are the angels of judgement and salvation. They speak as one because salvation and judgement are the two sides of the one divine reality. They remind the women of Jesus' saying, "The Son of Man must be handed over to sinners." Their presence declares him risen as Saviour and judge.

What is it, then, in Peter's words, to be "judge of the living and the dead" (Acts 10:42)? First, to be judge of all people, of every time and place, a judge of universal jurisdiction. The Christian tradition of Holy Saturday, based upon two passages from 1 Peter (3:18–20; 4:5–6), speaks of Jesus' salvation of those who died before his coming—with whom we should include all who have had no opportunity to know him. Second, to be "judge of the living and the dead" is to be judge of all those who, at his coming, will be living or dead. Christ is the judge at the end of history, to whom we must give an account. By our response to him we shall be judged. All this is to say that Jesus is Lord, "Lord of all"; the risen one on whom God has conferred his authority over all that is; the king reigning in God's kingdom until all his purposes are complete.

Jesus, the Son of Man, handed over to sinners, crucified and raised on the third day is, "The judge of the living and the dead". He was handed over to sinners, whose destiny is to die. We then, sinners who deserve to die, put to death him who did not deserve to die. We executed him as a sinner, for crimes against God and humanity—and God raised him. What more conclusive verdict could there be against humanity than to raise from the dead him whom we crucified? But through him, whom our self-interest crucified, God, who is compassionate and merciful, offers forgiveness and life. So the angels of judgement and mercy declare God's salvation in him.

The choice before us, then, is life in Christ or death. Many now simply believe that through death we all go to "a better place". While not denying God's mercy, this is neither the gospel nor the Christian faith. It is the human condition to die. "In Adam all die." It is God's will and gift in Christ that in him, "all shall be made alive" (1 Corinthians 15:22). But the whole gospel tradition is that to be part of this "all" requires the response of repentance and faith of all who are able to make it. The resurrection of Jesus is God's answer to the human condition. At death—as the critics of our hope point out—brain activity ceases. All that has sustained the personal life of this body stops. Except as we have failed to penetrate the mystery of human consciousness, there can be no continuity. But the same was true of Jesus, whose death is undisputed, who went to the same end as all of us, and who, on the third day, God raised from the dead. And, if God has raised Jesus, he will raise with him all who, by faith and baptism (incorporation into him in death) belong to him. Until then he reigns, as "judge of the living and the dead".

And if Jesus reigns with the authority of God over all that is, his rule involves the subjection of all other forces and forms of authority to himself (1 Corinthians 15:24–29), of which the last is death. Other powers—economic, social and political— rise and fall, come and go. Death remains, ultimate and absolute; or it did until God raised Jesus, the first fruits, the first-born of the dead, the first of all who belong to him. Death remains, indeed—difficult, fearful, often painful—but for those who are Christ's it is neutralized. Death's sting has been drawn; it can no longer separate us either from God or from those whom we love, because in Christ our connectedness remains. In him, "the bond of love is never broken".*

What of us, standing with those women that first Easter morning? Our critics might ask indeed, "Why look for the living among the dead?" Only our lives can disprove this. Or again, how shall we look for the living when so many of our congregations are grandparents, and the future of so many communities of faith is in doubt? But the pattern of Christian life is death and resurrection. Who knows what God will do with a congregation that is faithful? Even its death is not beyond God's purposes. Until then, however, its very existence is witness to Jesus' resurrection—perhaps an insignificant bunch of people, a tiny proportion of the population of the area, none better than anyone else, yet who stubbornly persist in keeping Sunday differently from the rest of the week because it is the day of the resurrection. And witnesses to Jesus' resurrection we are: we eat and drink with him this Easter morning.

---

* A line from a prayer in the Funeral Service of the Church of Ireland, *The Book of Common Prayer*, 2004, p. 492.

… The Passion according to John

Introduction

If we owe to Mark the very concept of a Gospel, we have in John's the culmination of its purpose (20:31). Jesus, whose identity as Son of God Mark traces to the moment of his baptism, and whom Matthew and Luke portray as constituted by the Spirit of God, is for John nothing less than the incarnation of God's eternal Word, the creating and redeeming embodiment of God. Instead of events and teaching collected and variously put into order by Mark, Matthew and Luke, John gives us a sustained and penetrating presentation of the person of Jesus, using a selection of "signs" (2:11; 4:54; 6:14 etc.), personal encounters, e.g. Nicodemus (3:1–10) and the Samaritan woman (4:1–26), and controversy with the authorities of Israel's temple. More than the other evangelists, John shows everything through the perspective of Jesus' death and resurrection. Jesus of Nazareth is the one who has risen from the dead. All that he says and does is seen in this light. Several times in the sermons that follow I have used the kaleidoscope as a metaphor for John's writing, in which themes and events familiar from the other Gospels are given a twist and seen in a new and sharply illuminating pattern.

John's narrative of the Passion begins immediately after Jesus' raising of Lazarus, in chapters 12 and 13, pausing for the "farewell discourses" and prayer of chapters 14 to 17, before moving to Jesus' arrest, trial and crucifixion in chapters 18 and 19. The events are, of course, and in all essentials, those of Mark, Matthew and Luke, but John's attention to symbolism and detail, his own theological language and allusions to the Hebrew scriptures, and sheer penetrating insight result in a narrative of extraordinary depth and power. It is no coincidence that in churches that use the Revised Common Lectionary the Passion according to John is read annually on Good Friday, after those by Matthew, Mark and Luke in succeeding years on Palm Sunday. In this, John brings us to the heart of the gospel. The incarnation reaches its fulfilment in the revelation of God in the crucified body of Jesus, in that "lifting up" which is at once his death and his exaltation to the godhead whose glory he reveals and whose embodiment he is. In all this, a light is shone upon "the world", human society as we know it, from which none of us can escape.

Preparing for Death

2 2

A preview of the Passion

John 12:1-11　　　　　　　　　　*Monday in Holy Week*

It should have been a lovely occasion: Jesus' friends had laid on a dinner for him. Not only were there bonds of mutual love; one of them, Lazarus, Jesus had raised from the dead. Mary's grief had prompted him to do it. Martha had already confessed him as the Christ. In Jesus they had seen the glory of God. It should have been an evening of thanksgiving and joy. But all around was menace. Goaded by his raising of Lazarus, the chief priests were plotting Jesus' death and had put the word out for his arrest. Bethany was a dangerous place for him. Next day he would ride into Jerusalem. With six days to go before Passover, the climax of the nation's calendar, this must mean a confrontation with the leaders who so bitterly opposed him.

In this meal, then, we see what is to come. Judas is present. Mary performs a gesture of which we have heard in the other Gospels, but to which John attributes particular significance. John says twice that Jesus is present as having raised Lazarus from the dead. Jesus is present as "the resurrection and the life"; he had given life to Lazarus and this must cost him his own life. "Except a seed fall into the earth and die" (12:24). The story of Lazarus is heavy with echoes of his own death: the anguish, the struggle, the shout, the stone, the tomb. So, in this meal, John gives us a preview and an interpretation of what is to come: a meal; a betrayal; death and burial—and something else too.

John describes Mary's anointing of Jesus. We have heard the story before. Mark (and Matthew) tell of an unknown woman anointing Jesus at Bethany, pouring ointment on his head. Luke tells, much earlier, of a woman of some notoriety anointing his feet, weeping, washing his feet with her tears and drying them with her hair. John tells of Mary, whom Jesus loves, anointing his feet with ointment that would cost a working man's wages for a year. Mary's is a gesture of love, an act of sacrifice and a mark of homage. Mary anoints Jesus as Messiah—but his feet, not his head—a Messiah in death. Her gesture points, as he says, to the day of preparation for his burial—that is, the day of his death. This is the Messiah who reigns from the tree.

Strangely, John tells us about this in advance. Mary's anointing is first described at the beginning of the story of the raising of Lazarus (11:2). She has done it in advance of his burial. This is Mary's response to Jesus' death, her thanksgiving for the death by which he has saved her brother, and will save her too. Mary's gesture is an identification with Jesus in his sacrifice. Its fragrance fills the house as the fragrance of sacrifice filled the temple. So, too, will the fragrance of Jesus' sacrifice fill the world. Six days later, at another meal, Jesus will wash his disciples' feet and dry them with the towel tied around his waist, drawing them to himself. He must wash them, cleanse them by his death, else they have no part with him. He must wash us all—and the feet, the dirty bits, stand for the whole. Mary's anointing of Jesus is her identification with him in his death, and demands of us too that we give our all to him.

But Judas is present, one of the twelve, the chosen, about to betray him. Judas sees not love but money; it is his motivation. He thinks of value, not of worth. He is one of us, to whom money matters, who inhabit a culture of value. We don't have to be a thief, but if money rules where love should, Caesar's coin instead of God's, we too betray the Lord. If we "measure" our compassion or stint our love, we are closer to Judas than to Mary. Judas is there in the Gospels to remind us of who we are.

But what of the plot to kill Lazarus, because he drew so many to Jesus? Nowhere else in the Gospels is it suggested that anyone else was as much as arrested with Jesus. What, then, shall we make of this? Jesus had raised Lazarus from the dead, the first of millions whose encounter with Jesus has been life-giving—so much so that they might describe the transformation in terms of resurrection, new life, being raised from the dead. Those whose own lives and words testify to Jesus as the resurrection and the life are his most compelling witnesses. It is his life in them that speaks. All through history they have been watched, harassed and persecuted by those whose interest is to maintain the status quo. Lazarus stands for many whose taste of the resurrection has put their own life on the line. Many have died in this faith.

In the dinner at Bethany, John gives us a glimpse of what is to come—a last supper, betrayal, death and burial. But this is not the last word. Jesus is present as the resurrection and the life; Lazarus as one whom he has raised from the dead; Martha as one who has confessed the Christ; Mary as one whose love has identified her with him in his death. This is Jesus' family, the infant Church, gathered around him. And this little dinner points to something else—to that final banquet of Jesus with his friends, when Judas will no longer be present. The only currency will be that of love, and there will be feasting and joy in the common life of the risen Christ for all whom Jesus has made his own.

2 3

The agony

John 12:20–36 *Tuesday in Holy Week*

John's Gospel is like a kaleidoscope. It takes familiar details of the story, turns them around, puts them together in a new pattern, shows them in a new light, and invites us to see more of the truth of Christ. So it is here. Jesus has just entered Jerusalem. We should now expect to hear of his cleansing of the temple. Instead, some Greeks arrive! Then we hear of Jesus wrestling with his destiny, not in Gethsemane but in public, and days before the Last Supper. If we ask why John should so change the story, it is to show us more of the significance of Jesus and, above all, of his death.

John also uses, however, a language of his own—just as the pieces in the kaleidoscope change colour when it is turned. John speaks of the "hour" of Jesus. He means the decisive moment in Jesus' life, for which everything else has been a preparation. But, as Jesus is Israel's Messiah, the Son of God and Saviour of the world, this is also the decisive moment in history, the hinge on which all else turns. Jesus' "hour" is the moment of his crucifixion, of the judgement of this world's order, and the beginning of the new creation, the inauguration of the kingdom of God. Three times in this passage Jesus says, "Now". His hour has come. But "now", too, is the moment of our decision: to accept the cross and all it entails, or to refuse; the moment of our judgement.

The second word of John's special language is "glory", and "glorifying". Glory denotes what God is, God in God's self—glorious. For Jesus to be "glorified" is to be revealed as he is, the very embodiment of God. But glory is God's, by definition. Jesus is glorified only as he does God's will, a will which is also his own. So Jesus is never glorified, except by God as the consequence of his obedience. The supreme moment of Jesus' glory, the ultimate revelation of God in him, is his death upon the cross.

Jesus, then, has entered Jerusalem. Instead, however, of his taking over the temple, John tells of a complicated little ballet involving some Greeks, Philip and Andrew, whose names are Greek, who both come from Bethsaida, of whom we first heard at the beginning of the Gospel (1:40-41,43-44). Both had immediately brought someone else to Jesus, Andrew first finding Peter and then Philip Nathanael. The Greeks want to "see" Jesus. This marks a new beginning. To "see" Jesus, in John's language, is to come to him, to know him. The Greeks represent the world beyond the God-centred life of Judaism; the world of science, thought and philosophy; in contemporary terms the secular world. Their recognition of Jesus as Israel's Messiah marks the beginning of the world's conversion to God. They are the equivalent of Matthew's "wise men from the east" worshipping the new-born king of the Jews (Matthew 2:1). In coming to Jesus, they fulfil the purpose for which the temple was built, as "a house of prayer for all nations" (Isaiah 56:7; Mark 11:17). For this, Jesus reclaimed it, and it was this challenge to its priestly authorities which set in train his Passion and death.

Jesus' answer to the Greeks' request is, "The hour has come for the Son of Man to be glorified." The only way that the world as a whole can recognize Israel's God is through her crucified Messiah. Only so can the barriers of exclusiveness and superiority be broken down. Only so can the world be saved. Jesus speaks of his death in terms of a seed of wheat, the life-giving grain of the world. Unless it is buried in the earth and "dies", becoming part of the earth, its resources exhausted in creating new life—the purpose of its existence—it remains alone, encased in its husk. To bear fruit, the seed must break out and cease to be what it is. Just so Jesus, the Son of Man, the human being, must die and be broken out of the kernel of Judaism, to bring life—abundant, endlessly multiplied—to the world.

Jesus says that it is the same for us, especially in our individualistic age. If we don't "hate" our own life, that is "die" and move on from where we started, we too shall remain alone. If "what we have we hold", each in our own little husk, each the centre of our own little world, we fail to fulfil the purpose of our existence and there is nothing more for us. It is willingness to "die", to let go, to give oneself, to be changed, that opens the way to love. To die for the beloved is the ultimate act of love, and love is the way from isolation and self-centredness into community, relatedness and co-operation; into the bearing of much fruit. It is tempting, of course, to point to others living for themselves and to the consequences. It is, however, important in today's interconnected world to recognize the consequences of nations living for themselves, limited by their own self-interest, and the death which this threatens for so many. Most difficult of all may be the recognition of the extent of our own self-centredness, the desire to protect our own interests and the "pull" with which these can manipulate our political and national life.

And again, says Jesus, "whoever serves me must follow me". To serve Jesus is to acknowledge him as our Lord, to see ourselves not as our own but his. To follow him means being prepared to fall into the ground and die; to be stripped of our husks, to lose ourselves in lives committed in love. "Where I am, there shall my servant be"—and not necessarily in glory!* We must never forget that we follow a man who gave everything and was crucified. This is the basis of whatever we call him or say of him. On this is founded his identity as our Lord and ours as his people. There is no place in the Christian faith for personal glory or advantage. Honour is the Father's gift for those who have followed his Son.

But before glory comes agony, anguish, the cost of obedience. "Now is my soul troubled. And what should I say, 'Father, save me from this hour'? No, it is for this reason that I came to this hour." This is the climax of Jesus' life and destiny, and of the history of the world. The agony and the ignominy of the cross are beyond our imagination, but for Jesus to be spared it would be to reject God's purpose for the world and for him. It would also be to reject his very identity as the embodiment of the Father. "Father, glorify your name" means "Your will be done"—as Jesus had done it in everything. The voice that answers, "I have glorified it, and will glorify it again"—John is using his kaleidoscope again—is the voice at Jesus' baptism: "This is my beloved Son, in whom I am well pleased." The Son is beloved for his obedience, his absolute at-one-ness with the

---

*   Contrast the lines in the well-known hymn by John E. Bode, "O Jesus, I have promised": "that where thou art in glory, there shall thy servant be".

Father. God has been glorified as Jesus has revealed his presence in all that he has said and done, from changing water into wine at Cana to raising Lazarus of Bethany. All are signs of the new life, ultimately poured out through the cross, whose hour has now come. God will finally be glorified, revealed in his truth, in the death, resurrection and ascension of Jesus, and in the gift of the Spirit.

The "lifting up of the Son of Man" is at once Jesus' brutal execution and the exaltation of the Son of God to reign in the sovereignty of suffering love. As, therefore, Jesus is crucified, the world is judged in its rejection and destruction of the Son of God. A world that prefers its own darkness and its own way of going renounces the light, determines its own destiny. "The ruler of this world is cast out" as Christ ascends the cross to reign as Lord. The tempter, who panders to our self-centredness with delusions of our self-sufficiency, is exposed. He who is crucified will become the temple of God, drawing all people to himself with nothing but love. He is himself the "place" where God is to be found and where sin is forgiven, in the truth of a love that has given everything for us.

2 4

The death blow

John 13:21-32 *Wednesday in Holy Week*

The betrayal of Jesus is a death blow. From this moment, in the sardonic language of Death Row, Jesus is a "dead man walking". This is why, in the language explored above, Jesus can say after Judas' departure, "Now the Son of Man has been glorified . . . ". The die is cast. Nothing can now prevent the fulfilment of God's purpose. "Glory" is John's word for God's presence in Jesus, visible in its fullness when, in complete identity of will and purpose with the Father, Jesus is crucified. From this moment of betrayal, God's glory shines in him.

Jesus' betrayal is also the death blow in the sense that it is this that hands him over to death. Without this, the plotting of Jesus' enemies would be useless. Without this, there would be no arrest, examination by religious leaders, no trial before Pilate, no abuse, no mockery, no crucifixion—and no salvation of the world. The whole movement towards the crucifixion of the Son of God begins from within the circle and begins with Jesus. It is only so that the enemy within, the Satan, the tempter, ever present and the most dangerous of all, can be overcome.

Jesus knows that this is the death blow. He is "troubled in spirit" as he declares that one of his own will betray him. His words are the same as in Mark and Matthew, as is the confusion that follows. No one knew of whom he was speaking. No one suspected the presence of a traitor. In Mark's account, Jesus adds, "one who is eating with me", and he answers his disciples' questions with, "It is one of the twelve, one who is dipping bread into the dish with me." The traitor, then, is one of the chosen, one of the circle who shares in the table fellowship. But all were dipping bread into the dish with Jesus. His words have not identified the traitor.

It could have been any of them. None of them knew—not even, perhaps, in Mark's account, Jesus himself.

John, however, says that Jesus tells one intimate disciple, "It is the one to whom I give the morsel when I have dipped it." Here, Jesus knows the traitor's identity. He has for some time: "Did I not choose you, the twelve? Yet one of you is a devil" (6:70). In this Gospel, Jesus' sovereignty extends to his knowing all things, as God knows, from whom nothing is hidden. For John, Jesus' sovereignty is undiminished by his Passion. It is he who initiates it, and he who is in charge throughout, the judge of those who judge him, who reigns as he is crucified. What, then, is Jesus doing as he dips the morsel and gives it to Judas?

Notice, first, the solemnity of it all, introduced by Jesus' words, "Verily, verily, I say unto you . . .", as the King James Bible puts it. The traitor, too, is fully identified for us, for the first time in this Gospel, as "Judas, son of Simon Iscariot". Jesus dips a morsel, a little piece of food, not necessarily bread, and gives it to him. A little earlier in the supper, Jesus adapted a line of Psalm 41 to say, "He who eats my bread has lifted his heel against me." This is about more than treachery. Jesus has also said (6:54), "He who eats my flesh . . . has eternal life . . . ." Hence the ambiguous word, "morsel", used four times. In giving it to Judas, Jesus is giving himself into Judas' hands—himself the Bread of Life; himself the Passover Lamb. Jesus is inaugurating his Passion that will bear fruit in the salvation of the world.*

All this is in the context of the Last Supper, that gathering of the chosen which is the origin of the Church's first act of worship. The traitor, then, is one of us. He eats, as Jesus says, his bread—but not his flesh. He is one whose feet Jesus has washed—yet who, as Jesus says, is not clean (13:10,11). Here at the heart of the community of Jesus is evil, totally concealed. The traitor's identity remains hidden even as Jesus tells him, "'What you are going to do, do quickly.' No one at the table knew why Jesus said this to him." The traitor is unrecognized. Except for what has been revealed to one privileged witness, it could have been any of them.

---

* John includes nothing of Judas' kiss to identify Jesus at his arrest. In John's account, Jesus' gift of the morsel to Judas is the equivalent moment in the story—in this case a genuine act of love in which Jesus gives himself into Judas' hands.

They thought, says John, that Jesus was telling him to buy what they needed for the festival or to give something to the poor. As John told us at Mary's anointing of Jesus (12:4-6), Judas had the purse and he said that the ointment should have been sold for the benefit of the poor. The point is that Judas was trusted. The first half that verse of Psalm 41, which Jesus quoted above, reads, "Even my bosom friend in whom I trusted". He was the treasurer, a position involving a particular trust, greater than any other. His stealing (12:6) was also hidden. Giving to the poor was a mark of piety. Was this something at which Judas excelled? Judas was the last person anyone would expect to betray Jesus.

And perhaps we can go a little further. Having received the morsel, Judas knew what he had to do. He went out to do it with a good conscience. He had received the Lord's morsel, a mark of his favour. Surely he had the Lord's authority and blessing. Did he even think that he was his most loyal servant, even entrusted with his commission? He had eaten the supper. His feet had been washed. He was one of Jesus' own. He was, surely, certain of himself and blind to his evil. Satan had entered into him, says John, taken him over without his knowledge. Evil, real evil, is secret, masked, disguised and hidden, not least from ourselves. As Judas went out, it may have been under the illusion of his own perfection as Jesus' disciple. That is diabolical. Judas was not a spy, consciously working for some external authority. Under the guise of loyalty Judas, son of Simon Iscariot, was working for himself.

It is now almost a commonplace that people who were abused as children felt unable to tell anyone because they were sure that they would not be believed. Their abuser was trusted, a pillar of the community, even of the congregation. Abuse is always secret and, far from recognizing their wrong, abusers may believe that what they are doing is good. We are not all abusers, but we are all more conscious of our better parts than of our faults. We all believe in our own goodness and are blind to the evil within. There is a Judas in all of us. That is why he is a universal figure, and why we always point to him in somebody else.

We betray Jesus when, as his people, we act under some other authority, believing we do right. Then the tempter has conned us. It happens when we put money, self, fears, position, personal advantage, party, community, economic system or whatever before Jesus and his command to love. Anything omitted from that list may be a sin of mine to which I am particularly blind. It is not that these things are necessarily bad in themselves—even fears have their place. Rather, when as Christians we are swayed by these things to take a way other than Christ's, and believe we do well, we betray Jesus. This is sin, and it is serious.

After receiving the morsel, Judas went out; out of the circle of love, the fellowship, the community of the redeemed; into the darkness, into the night. "Woe," says Jesus in Mark, "to that man by whom the Son of Man is betrayed. It would be better for that man if he had not been born." The Gospels, each in their own way, show Judas, son of Simon Iscariot, to have gone by his own choice into outer darkness, cut off from Christ's redemption. Judas has gone where none of us would wish to follow. Yet it was through the act that began with Judas' betrayal that the world was redeemed. Why, then, is Judas condemned? Jesus himself not only foresaw but set in motion that act and accepted its consequence. Since, too, the betrayal came from within the circle of his own, his own are included among those for whom Jesus died. We are all of us, friend and foe of the Lord alike, on an absolute equality in our sin. If Judas was different, is it that he thought he wasn't?

2 5

No greater love

John 13:1–17   *Thursday in Holy Week, Maundy Thursday*

John tells us little of the Last Supper; he knew all about it. Jesus is, for him, the bread of life, and uses language more violent than in any other Gospel: "Unless you eat the flesh of the Son of Man and drink his blood, you have no life in you" (6:53).* Salvation is in Christ, and nowhere else. Instead, at the supper, John tells of Jesus' great acted parable, that foreshadows all that is to come and declares what it means. This parable, too, enacts some of Jesus' most troubling words, "I am among you as one who serves" (Luke 22:27) and "whoever wishes to be first among you must be the slave of all. For the Son of Man came not to be served but to serve, and to give his life a ransom for many" (Mark 10:44,45).

Jesus' "hour" has come—that climax of his life for which everything else has been preparation. The Passover is at hand, the great feast of liberation. "The devil had already made up his mind that Judas should betray him" is what the best text of the Greek says. The enemy, the enemy within, has laid his plans, plans which are yet within the knowledge and purpose of God. Jesus' cross will be the Passover of the world, his "hour" the conquest of evil and the world's liberation from its grip, as the glory of God shines in his Son, humbled as one of us to a criminal's death.

So Jesus lays down his garments, as he will lay down his life. Our clothes express who we are. He takes water and, one by one, washes his disciples' feet. He dries them with the towel tied around him, the dress

---

*   The crude materiality of these words is paralleled by Thomas' demand for a tangible exploration of Jesus' wounds (20:25). Both are about the reality of encounter with the risen Lord.

91

of a slave. He leaves nothing unfinished. He loves them to the end. But why the towel tied around him, when one over the arm would be so much easier? Like this, he draws them to himself (12:32), their body to his, as he kneels beside each one reclining at the table. "This is my body, given for you." "This is my blood, shed for you"—the blood of sacrifice that cleanses, restores and makes whole, the blood of the Lamb of God. Water and towel, bread and wine, body and blood: Jesus enacts the Eucharist and what it means. He loves us to the end, to the uttermost. He loves us to perfection: his death will present us to God. He loves us to bits, to bring us home to the kingdom.

But Peter will have none of it—Peter, the leader, our representative in our best intentions to be faithful. Peter is scandalized, as he was when Jesus first foretold his death: "God forbid it, Lord! This must never happen to you!" (Matthew 16:22). Replying, Jesus called him "Satan"—thinking the way we think. That a master should do the work of a slave is an offence to the social order. Only later will Peter understand, when the cross has shown him Jesus' meaning. Unless we too connect it with the cross, Jesus' *example* in dying for us, we too shall misunderstand. Unless, like Peter, Jesus washes us; unless Jesus dies for us, we do not belong to him; we have no part in his kingdom. Jesus' dialogue with Peter is his dialogue with us. We must be humbled, as Jesus has humbled himself for us; been dishonoured, humiliated, abused beyond our imagination; made into sin (2 Corinthians 5:21) to bring us to God.

Peter, however, still doesn't quite understand. If not to be washed is to be cut off from the Lord, Peter wants to be washed all over! But, in washing the feet, Jesus washes the dirty bits; the sore, hardened and calloused bits; the deformed and twisted bits; the tired, aching and weary bits, to present us to God unstained, unblemished. Nothing further is needed. At the cross we are bathed in Christ's love, "washed by the Holy Spirit and made clean"* as never before. In baptism, we are identified with Jesus in his death and resurrection—and baptism is properly by total immersion, a drowning, a bathing of the whole body. Yet, as we know, baptism is not the end of our sin. Sin is a daily reality in our lives. Our

---

*   From the Baptism Service of the Church of Ireland, *The Book of Common Prayer*, 2004, p. 358.

feet have still to be washed, repeatedly. So we come, week by week, to dine with our Lord, that he may do for us what is necessary.

After the washing, Jesus resumes his clothes and his place, to speak to us as our teacher and Lord. If he has washed our feet, we are to wash one another's feet. We are to do as he has done for us, who died for us. We are to be prepared to die for one another as our way of life. "Servants are not greater than their master." The humility and love of Jesus' death for us is to be the mark of our living with one another. "Messengers are not greater than him who sent them." Humility and service are to be the marks of our living with those around us, so that he can draw them also to himself. And this is not theory but practice: "If you know these things, blessed are you if you do them."

We wash one another, therefore, in forgiveness. As the community of the forgiven, we are to forgive. This is the hallmark of our life in Christ, and the key to our unity in him and to our mission as Christians. Forgiveness is to be our way of life, despite all the myriad ways in which we hurt one another, neglect one another or take each other for granted. Might it be the practice of forgiveness that makes a Christian marriage Christian? There is joy and life in forgiveness—in humility. It is humbling to ask forgiveness; humbling to realize that the person of whom I ask forgiveness is better than I. For the one who forgives, it is humbling to let go of the offence, to bury the wounded pride, and to embrace as a fellow sinner a brother or sister.

But if Christ is among us as one who serves, he sends us as servants also, to serve others as he has served us. This is our priesthood, our service in him to the world that he came to save. If, then, our service is modelled on his, there will be nothing that we will not do. We know of those whose extraordinary faithfulness and sacrifice are examples to us in our generation. We should begin, however, with the little things nearer home. It is the willingness in love to do the difficult thing, to go to the difficult place, to have the difficult conversation, to meet with difficult company, that is the essence of Christian service. We shall be humbled. We shall find ourselves inadequate. We shall be stripped of our illusions of our goodness and our competence. It is a way of dying, but it is the way of life, manifesting, however dimly, the glory of Christ to those who do not know him; following him who gave his life for us; Christ who is our life; Jesus, our Lord.

2 6

He gave himself

John 18:1–11 *Tuesday in Holy Week*

In John's account of the Passion, as we saw above, Jesus himself sets in motion the process that will lead to his death. Knowing that Judas will betray him, he sends him out to do it. The Greek word in all the Gospels that we translate as "betray" also carried the neutral meanings of to give up or to hand over. Here, then, we see how Jesus gives himself up and hands himself over to his Passion.

Again, John tells a familiar story differently: no mention here of Gethsemane; no agonized prayer; no kiss from Judas, and the disciples don't run away. John includes other things about the place of arrest, and of a surprisingly large arresting squad. The bones of the story are as we know them but are fleshed out differently. John's subject is the Word made flesh, whose arrest is all of a piece with his cross.

John sets the scene; when Jesus crosses the Wadi Kidron he crosses the city boundary, like David during Absalom's rebellion against him (2 Samuel 15:23). Jesus and his disciples enter what John alone calls a garden. John also tells of a garden at the place of crucifixion (19:41)— outside the city, where Jesus was buried. Betrayal—cross—resurrection: each is inseparable from the other; Maundy Thursday to Easter Sunday represent one celebration of God's salvation. Judas brings to this place, literally, a cohort of soldiers—six hundred men! With them are the temple police (more literally, servants) from the chief priests and Pharisees. In a strange alliance, the nationalist Pharisees are aligned with the compromising priests, and all are in league with the Romans. The world unites against Jesus: Jews and Gentiles; Rome and Jerusalem; the rulers of the world and the guardians of the faith. They come with lanterns, torches and weapons—at the full moon of Passover! These are the people of the night, with Judas who went out into the night (13:30). Their lights and weapons are those of people who walk in darkness—blind to the light of the world.

Jesus comes out, out of the garden, and interrogates the party: "Whom are you looking for?" "Jesus, the Nazarene"—Jesus, the consecrated one. They have come to arrest Messiah! His own people have gone over to their enemies. Jesus replies, "I am he." He discloses himself, and exposes Judas, standing with the men of darkness. No kiss is possible. Judas had to come, but only to show them the place. They cannot, however, seize Jesus; they draw back and fall to the ground. Jesus has uttered the Name, "I am". Their weaponry is powerless against God's Anointed. The divine presence is unbearable to those who are not reconciled to him, who are not his own. Instead of Jesus falling to the ground in prayer, John has his captors falling powerless before him. John is affirming the sovereignty of Jesus, the work of the cross, the judgement of the world.

There is nothing more for Judas to do. Jesus "betrays" himself, hands himself over. He must be betrayed from within his circle, but he hands himself over. The New Testament witnesses that "God did not spare his own Son but gave him up for us all" (Romans 8:32). It records also that Jesus handed himself over: "The Son of God who loved me and gave himself for me" (Galatians 2:20); who, "gave himself up for us" (Ephesians 5:2); who, "committed himself to him who judges justly" (1 Peter 2:23). Through all the squalor of the Passion there shines the grace-filled purpose of God in Christ, giving himself for the life of the world.

First, too, Jesus saves his own: "If you are looking for me, let these go." The Good Shepherd lays down his life for the sheep. The shepherd is struck, but the sheep are not scattered. They are in the garden, in the fold, the place of salvation, close to the cross. None would be lost of all who were given to him. So he said at the supper (17:12), and as the bread of life (6:39). The Church is founded at the cross and needs no other protection.

But someone had a sword and used it: he cut off the high priest's slave's ear. John and Luke agree that it was the right ear, but John alone names Peter and the slave as Malchus, and John says that Peter *mutilated* his right ear. A slave was his master's property, and his master's right ear was anointed with blood at his consecration as high priest. Symbolically, his master is being disqualified from office; the old religion superseded as it condemns Jesus. John's Jesus does not heal the servant (contrast Luke 22:51). Judgement is at work. This is the significance of Jesus' crossing the Kidron: the divine presence is leaving the city.

But why Peter? No other Gospel names him here, although all four Gospels record Jesus' rebuke. All three, however, record that when Peter himself first recognized Jesus—the Messiah!—Jesus immediately foretold his Passion: "Undergo great suffering . . . be rejected by the elders, the chief priests, and the scribes . . . be killed, and after three days rise again" (Mark 8:31; cf. Matthew 16:21; Luke 9:22). Peter would have none of this, and Jesus rebuked him, "Get behind me, Satan!" (Mark 8:33). There is no talk of Satan here—Judas belongs to him—but God's purpose is still the same, and Peter is still trying to thwart it: "The cup which the Father has given me, shall I not drink it?" So John echoes Jesus' prayer in Gethsemane (Mark 14:36). God's will is that Jesus hand himself over, that he be crucified. Peter, who resisted Jesus' washing his feet, still hasn't got it, persisting in his own will and strength. He will die for Jesus, not Jesus for him! That Jesus gave himself for us is understood only from the Holy Spirit.

27

Conviction

John 18:12–27 *Wednesday in Holy Week*

John proclaims Jesus' sovereignty even in his arrest. His betrayal, his handing over to death, is God's will. Peter, resisting his arrest, is attempting to frustrate God's will. As in the other Gospels, Peter's involvement continues: as Jesus goes for trial, so does he. But when it comes to Jesus' trial before the priests, John's account is peculiar. There is no question, "Are you the Christ, the Son of the Blessed?"; no witnesses, false or otherwise; no verdict. John paints his own picture of familiar events so that we might see Jesus, and ourselves, in a new light.

The trial begins with Jesus already bound. Already he is guilty. The whole of John's Gospel is about Jesus' identity as the Messiah, the Christ, the Son of God. For five chapters (5, 7–10) Jesus and the Jewish leadership have argued it out. Jesus has already been tried, and Caiaphas has already condemned him (11:49–50), "It is expedient that one man should die for the people ...". This, then, is a show trial, and worse: Caiaphas is the high priest, but proceedings are in the house of Annas, his father-in-law and former high priest. Yet, "the high priest" conducts the interrogation and it ends as Jesus is sent—bound, guilty—to Caiaphas. The confusion is deliberate. The mutilation of the high priest's servant symbolized the disqualification of the high priest from office as the Messiah was arrested on his orders. Now, therefore, neither Caiaphas nor Annas is high priest. The court is self-appointed and a fraud. No one has authority to try the anointed of God.

It is not, therefore, Jesus who is on trial, but the court. True, he is asked about his disciples and his teaching. He says nothing about the disciples: the answer is being given outside. But he declares that his teaching has always been open, in synagogue and temple where all Jews congregate. He has been the true shepherd of Israel, in his place with his people. But this is a hearing in secret, a kangaroo court, where he is being invited to incriminate himself. The court should properly ask those who heard him, seek witnesses—due process—witnesses to the truth. The court, however, wants none. Perhaps there are none. Jesus stands alone; his nation has rejected him.

Jesus' demand for justice is met with a slap in the face. Unlawful authority is upheld by violence, as Jesus himself is repudiated. So the court condemns itself. The issue is fundamental, right or wrong, good or evil? "If I have spoken wrongly, testify to the wrong; but if rightly, why do you strike me?" The court has chosen evil. As Jesus is sent, bound, to Caiaphas, the court, the priesthood of Israel, is convicted and disqualified. This is the verdict of the cross.

What, then, of the disciples, whose representative stands outside? John introduces two new figures, a woman who keeps the door, and another disciple, known (surprisingly?) to the high priest. So far, Peter has done well. He has followed Jesus. But at the door of Annas' house, he hesitates: this is enemy territory: no place for a disciple, except that Jesus is already there. The other disciple speaks for Peter and brings him in but the doorkeeper asks, "Aren't you also one of his disciples?" "I am not." Where Jesus said, "I am" and handed himself over, Peter says, "I'm not." He follows no further, in a place where the very presence of another disciple suggests that he was not necessarily at risk. Soon Peter is standing with the opposition around the fire, doing what comes naturally on a cold night, one of the crowd.

It gets worse. The men with whom Peter is standing repeat the question. Again, Peter says, "I'm not"—as Jesus had repeated his "I am." Peter is sinking. Then a witness appears, whose brother's ear Peter had cut off: "Didn't I see you with him in the garden?" (And the garden is, in fact, the place of safety, in which Jesus left the disciples.) Eyewitness testimony; incontrovertible evidence. Peter denies it and is convicted. He has denied the truth and denied his Lord. John says nothing about his remembering Jesus' words or weeping. Peter has condemned himself. Jesus stands alone as the cock crows.

Judas is a representative disciple, one of us. So is Peter. John connects them: Judas, son of Simon Iscariot and Simon Peter. Betrayal and denial: the two ways of breaking faith. The difference between them is that Judas *chose* the other side. He represents the terrible, secret risk of treachery in us, whose working is unnoticed until too late. Peter tried and failed. As Jesus said, Peter could not follow him (13:36–38)—until Jesus himself had died for him, until he had shown him the meaning of his washing of Peter's feet. The cross convicts us all. Betrayal and denial are always with us. We have no standing of our own. The cross convicts disciples no less than everyone else.

We cannot follow Jesus unless we are, in Paul's characteristic phrase, "in him" who died for us. The conviction that we are is the work of the Holy Spirit, the birthright of our baptism, of every Christian. No other gift is as precious. As Jesus' trial is inset in the story of Peter's trial, so now the two trials are one. The Lord is tried in his disciples. This is how he speaks to the world. Disciples are usually tried informally, involuntarily—in uncongenial company, unfriendly territory or gathered around the fire, looking after themselves. But where his people are, the Lord is, and his command is, "Speak openly; bear witness to the truth." In the much-quoted question, attributed to the late Hans Küng, "If you were on trial for being a Christian, would there be enough evidence to convict you?" For Jesus said, "Whoever denies me before others I also will deny before my Father in heaven" (Matthew 10:33). When we remain silent, or say, "I'm not" to his "I am", we deny him.

The Conviction of the World

2 8

The charge

John 18:28–32   *Monday in Holy Week*

Taken, bound, from Annas' house to Caiaphas, Jesus is immediately taken on to Pilate's headquarters, the Praetorium. Caiaphas himself is no longer of any significance. What follows is a courtroom drama. A judge presides—Pilate. Politically, he represents Rome: Empire, the system that rules the world, the civil and military authority over a subject people. Judicially, he represents the law, for which Rome was famous. He is the symbol of law and order. The accused is Jesus. The prosecution is described as "the Jews" who are, more precisely, the "chief priests", the temple authorities. They represent the Jewish nation, Israel, the chosen people—partly self-governing but subject to Rome.

There are, however, gaps in the cast. There is no jury. This is not a democratic court. The issues at stake are power, the fate of a nation, the destiny of the world. There is no defence. Jesus is alone. He can call no witnesses. Just before they brought him to court, his last disciple had denied him. But nowhere in this trial does Jesus defend himself—and this is a clue to the identity of the accused and to what is at stake. The things of God cannot be judged in a human court. Transcendence cannot be encompassed by human process. Most striking of all, therefore, is that there is no charge.

Where, then, are we in this courtroom drama? Are we the jury, listening to the arguments before reaching a decision? Yes, in so far as we shall hear a private discussion between Pilate and Jesus. But there is no jury in this trial. Pilate, the representative of law and order, will try to adopt a position of neutrality, shuttling between the accusers and the accused. We shall see where this leads him, for we are dealing here with the gospel of Jesus Christ, which allows no neutrality; we must decide for him or against him. Ultimately, it is we who are judged, by our own decision.

Therefore, if we cannot identify ourselves with Jesus or with Pilate, and there is no place in the story for an impartial jury, the only place for us within this drama is among the "Jews"—the temple authorities and their supporters. To place ourselves among the opponents of Jesus may seem shocking. Certainly, John's Gospel is deeply hostile to "the Jews"; a hostility which reflects the bitter controversy between the infant Church and the synagogues of John's day. By describing the temple authorities consistently as "the Jews", John makes them embody and represent the nation—the nation which has already disowned its Messiah. The hostility to "the Jews" in John's Gospel has played its part in twenty centuries of Christian anti-Semitism. Theologically, however, as God's chosen people, the Jews are the representatives before God of the nations of the world and not otherwise different from them. Of them is the Christ, the Saviour of the world. The Fourth Gospel seems almost to forget that Jesus was a Jew. It shows an unbridgeable gulf between him and his people. Let this alert us to the gulf between us and him, which he alone can cross. We call it sin.

So to "the charge". "If this man were not an evildoer, we would not have handed him over to you." "Take it from us, he's a bad 'un!" What sort of charge is that? No wonder Pilate replies, "Take him yourselves and judge him according to your law." This exchange, however, bears further examination. They call *Jesus* an evildoer. At 6 a.m. they have delivered him to the Praetorium, but they have stayed outside. Passover will begin tonight, and they mustn't defile themselves by going in. The Praetorium belongs to the Gentiles and Jesus is in it alone. Jesus has been driven out of the promised land into an unclean place. Jesus has been treated as a scapegoat, driven alone into the desert bearing the sins of the people (Leviticus 16). Jesus has been brought here from Caiaphas—the man who had advised that it was expedient that one man should die for the people (11:50). It was, too, for Aaron, Caiaphas' predecessor with whom the priesthood originated, symbolically to place the people's sin upon the head of the goat before sending it away into the wilderness.

John calls Jesus, "the Lamb of God", and the righteous of Israel would slaughter their lambs in the temple that afternoon, ready for Passover at sunset. The Passover Lamb celebrated God's redemption of Israel from Egypt; it had nothing to do with sin. But Jesus is, for John, "the Lamb of God who takes away the sin of the world" (1:29). He is Lamb and scapegoat rolled into one: God's greater liberation, redemption from sin. Here he is, driven out to die, bearing the sins of his people as they preserve their fitness to eat the Passover. In the mind of those who bring him to Pilate, he is crucified already. It is their sin—and ours—that he bears.

Pilate replies, "Take him yourselves and judge him according to your law." Pilate either sees this as an internal Jewish problem, or he sees their game and wants no part in it. Either way, he doesn't want to get involved. But the leaders of the temple immediately reveal their hand, "It is not lawful for us to put anyone to death." This may be true. Rome may have forbidden Israel's leaders the use of the death penalty. But they stoned Stephen for blasphemy, and Paul avoided appearing before their court. The leadership, however, needed Jesus dead. For Pilate to refuse them, to hand Jesus back, meant chaos and disaster. Jesus' popularity threatened their power, their system and their accommodation with the Roman Empire, an accommodation that Caiaphas had defended with his comment about the expediency of Jesus' death. Jesus' acceptance of the unacceptable threatened the life and soul of the nation. He didn't observe the boundaries of a holy people as they understood them. Vital national interests were at stake. They needed Jesus dead but couldn't do it themselves, so Rome must do it for them. Jesus must be crucified.

Jesus, of course, had seen this coming. His coming as Israel's Messiah involves more than accusations of blasphemy for which a man might be stoned. It involves the whole social and political order. This includes dethroning the powerful in favour of the rule of God and freedom for the poor. It involves welcoming home the outcasts. It means facing the nation with its sin. Jesus knew he must fail; that he must be treated as a rebel and "lifted up from the earth to draw all people to himself" (12:32). He must be lifted up in crucifixion, the punishment of Rome, the ruler of the world. He must become the victim of the world's injustice, of its failure to defend the innocent and convict the guilty. Vital national interests take precedence over everything else.

"Vital national interests" justify the closing of borders to refugees. "Vital national interests" justify the bombing of cities. "Vital national interests" justify the retention and renewal of nuclear weapons. "Vital national interests" justified the refusal to negotiate an agreement on climate change until the last moment. "Vital national interests" justify the writing of trade agreements in favour of the rich and failing to share crucial medical technology with the rest of the world. "Vital national interests"—"living within our means"—have justified privileging the interests of the elderly over the young, and the wealthy over the poor. None of us is exempt from this. To whatever extent we benefit, we are all involved. The system that crucifies Jesus makes him not a Jewish but the universal scapegoat. The Lamb of God bears the sin of the world.

29

The witness

John 18:33–40   *Tuesday in Holy Week*

The second scene of the courtroom drama takes place inside Pilate's headquarters, the Praetorium. Examining Jesus, Pilate immediately brings out into the open the charge left unspoken in his dialogue with the temple leadership, "Are you the king of the Jews?" On the lips of a Roman governor, such a title smacks of sedition and rebellion. It is also the charge under which Jesus would die, fastened to his cross above his head, "Jesus of Nazareth, the King of the Jews".

    Replying to Pilate, Jesus starts to examine him. Did you come to this yourself—as Peter had once done—or did others tell you? Are you, just possibly, one of mine or are you investigating me? Pilate gives the game away: "Am I a Jew?" Jesus cannot possibly be his king! In his words we hear the centuries of contempt of the Gentile for the Jew. It would take Jesus' death and resurrection to break that barrier. Ever since, however, rather than accepting our inheritance in him, Christians have fought shy of his Jewishness. We have made him in our image; we have pilloried and pogromed his people. Meanwhile, Pilate proceeds judicially: your own people have handed you over to me. What have you done to deserve their enmity?

    Jesus speaks first in the negative. "My kingdom is not of this world"— not of the world which Pilate knows and represents, in which power is sought, held and brokered; in which authority rests upon the power to coerce by courts, penalties and ultimately force of arms; the world in which God comes second, at best, to national interests and to our own. If Jesus' kingdom were of this world, he would have people in arms as Pilate had people in arms, like every state before and since. Jesus forswears not only the arms allowed by Number 37 of the (Anglican) Thirty-Nine Articles of Religion, but all the authority that they represent and which derives from them. The authority that Jesus exercises is never imposed on anyone. We have only to read Christian history to see how far short we have fallen.

In one thing, however, Jesus corrects Pilate. Pilate believes the Jewish leaders have handed Jesus over to him. But Jesus speaks of his followers fighting to save him from the Jews! Jesus is their prisoner, not Pilate's; their scapegoat, the one who dies for his people. Only as their king can Jesus fulfil Israel's place as the representative of the nations before God. Only as Israel's Messiah can he fulfil her destiny to bring light to the Gentiles (Genesis 12:2; Isaiah 49:6), salvation to the world. In this Pilate is a mere instrument, a tool of the Jewish leadership and unwittingly, like Cyrus of old (Isaiah 44:28–45:4), an instrument of God.

But a kingdom implies a king. Pilate is still interested, even if Jesus has disavowed anything Pilate could consider dangerous. "So you are a king?" Jesus now declares his kingship positively, but in terms beyond Pilate's understanding, and perhaps ours too. Jesus has come to bear witness to the truth—a truth that is not of this world, but that comes into the world with him and in him. This is the truth that stands beyond the world and yet sustains the world. In this truth there is no lie, nothing of evil, deceit or fraud; nothing of manipulation or seeking advantage; nothing of selfishness or of mixed motives. In this truth, there is nothing of sin and everything of God; nothing—only love. Jesus is the witness— the martyr—to this truth, which is nothing less than God. If, as the embodiment of God, Jesus will not take power on the world's terms, he must be the victim of those who do. Love is fulfilled in sacrifice, in a life laid down for friends and enemies. Jesus, crucified, is the way, the truth and the life. The glory of love is manifest at the cross, full of grace and truth (1:14). That Jesus' kingdom is not of this world is no invitation to otherworldliness, but to a disciplined, dedicated following of Jesus in the truth revealed at the cross. "Where I am, there shall my servant be" (12:26)—sacrificed!

"Everyone," says Jesus, "who is of the truth listens to my voice." This is the good shepherd, whose own sheep hear his voice, and who lays down his life for them. Here the witness challenges the judge. The interview is ending as it began, with Jesus questioning Pilate. "Do you hear my voice? Do you see the truth in me? Do you recognize in me an authority from which your own is ultimately derived?" Pilate turns away. "What is truth?" Power is what matters. In the Fourth Gospel, we are judged—and the world is judged—by our response to Jesus. We are faced with falsehood and truth, darkness and light. By our choice we judge ourselves. So Pilate is convicted. Where Jesus, the embodiment of truth is concerned, to choose neutrality is to stand against him.

The truth in all its glory, of course, is finally disclosed on the cross in the sacrifice of love. Pilate is but an agent of this disclosure. We, however, declare ourselves the heirs of this truth, born of water and the Spirit, born of God, sheep of the shepherd's flock. Whose voice, then, do we hear in our daily decisions?

Formally, however, Pilate has preserved his neutrality. He returns to the Jewish leadership outside. He finds no case to answer and proposes a face-saving formula. They have a custom that he should release someone for them at Passover. Would they accept the King of the Jews? "The King of the Jews"! Now the charge is in the open. Pilate proclaims Jesus the king of the Jews to his people. Pilate offers them their king—an offer they are bound to refuse! A nation must choose its own king, or else he is a puppet. The Pilate who could not see the truth has ensured his condemnation. They reject Jesus and choose a bandit. The good shepherd had spoken of those who preceded him, the rulers of Israel, as thieves and bandits (10:8). In a terrible piece of the irony characteristic of the Fourth Gospel, the rulers of his day choose one of their own.

Whom do we choose when the time comes? Seldom do we choose bandits literally. We do, however, choose people to represent our interests. We choose selfishly. This is democratic politics. The sharper the conflict—social, economic, inter-community, international—the greater the pressure to choose "one of our own" to defend our interests—never mind the common good. Amid recession, competition for resources, the effects (already) of a changing climate, and escalating inequality, politics has polarized, locally, nationally and internationally. Such polarization has happened before with terrible consequences. When we feel our interests threatened, we choose aggression. For all its advantages, democracy cannot bring in the kingdom of God. That kingdom is ruled by truth of another order—of sacrifice and love. To hear this truth means listening for the shepherd's voice—from the cross. Otherwise, we are at serious risk of choosing Barabbas.

30

The prisoner

John 19:1–7 *Wednesday in Holy Week*

When Jesus is rejected and Barabbas set free, the scene changes. Jesus is scourged—with a spiked whip—dressed up, mocked and struck in the face. What has become of Pilate's neutrality? It has been suggested that Pilate is trying to make Jesus an object of compassion, to secure his release. Luke, however, tells of mockery by Herod's soldiers. Mark and Matthew tell of Jesus scourged at the end of his trial, before the soldiers mock him and crucify him. Crucifixion began with scourging. Mark and Matthew record it in a phrase. It happened; it was awful, but incidental. John has brought the scourging and mockery into the heart of the trial and gives the scourging a whole sentence: "Then Pilate therefore took Jesus and scourged him." He did it himself. It is as brutal as that, and scourging before sentence is highly irregular.

If we look a little more closely, John, like Mark, tells of a crown of thorns and a purple robe. But he summarizes the soldiers' mock homage with the simple statement that they struck him on the face. John's word for scourging also differs from that used by Mark and Matthew. But his words for both scourging and striking are those in the Greek of Isaiah 50:6, the third song of the servant of God: "I gave my back to scourgings and my cheeks to strikings." John is inviting us to see in Jesus, scourged, mocked and struck the suffering servant of Isaiah, at once the prophet himself and a figure of faithful Israel. Isaiah's song, too, is about a trial, at which the servant will be vindicated.

So will Israel's faithful representative be vindicated? Certainly the soldiers perform their mock homage, "Hail, King of the Jews!"—again, the title on his cross. Gentiles mock the king and the nation he represents.

But they have dressed him in a parody of imperial splendour, acanthus leaves for the laurels of empire, and an emperor's purple robe. John asks us to look at all this through the lens of the cross and of the earliest convictions of Christian faith. Here in the Praetorium—Gentile territory in Israel—are the unwitting representatives of the Gentiles who would pay homage to Jesus, crucified and risen, in faith and hope. They are even, in fact, the first representatives of the nations who, in the fulfilment of her hope, would flock to Jerusalem to worship Israel's God (e.g. Zechariah 8:20–23). In Jesus is fulfilled God's choice of Israel to bring light to the nations, salvation to the ends of the earth. To him is all dominion given, on earth and in heaven. Pilate has scourged him; the soldiers have abused him; together they will crucify him. He will reign over all. This is the conviction of the world.

The trial then resumes. Pilate goes out to the temple leadership to announce Jesus' appearance, "to let you know that I find no case to answer"—his second declaration of Jesus' innocence. Jesus comes out with his crown and purple robe, and Pilate presents him to his people: "Behold, the man." He is no longer, "The King of the Jews", whom they have rejected, but "The man", whom they brought at the beginning of the day on unspecified charges. Now, here he is, crowned and robed, their king in parody. Here, again, is John's savage irony. In her mock king, Pilate is mocking the people Israel, whose terrible destiny it has been, biblically and historically, to be mocked and despised among the nations from the time of the exile until Messiah comes. Here is Israel's Messiah, mocked—and he has warned us that his own must share his destiny.

But again there is more. Pilate presents as "The man" he who spoke of himself as "The Son of Man". In the Gospel, the Son of Man ascends to heaven as he first descended from heaven (3:13). He must be lifted up—crucified—to draw all people to himself (3:14; 12:34). He gives the food that endures to eternal life. His flesh must be eaten and his blood drunk (that is, we must participate in his sacrifice) to partake of this life (6:27,53). His hour has now come to be glorified (12:23)—lifted up on the cross to the Father. Lifted up, he is honoured with the Father's Name, "I am" (8:28) and given authority to execute judgement (5:22)—the authority which is God's alone. Pilate presents us with a humiliation. Faith sees in it he who, in suffering, reigns from the tree.

Now Jesus is rejected in person: "Crucify! Crucify!" Again, what was unspoken at the beginning is now in the open. So the conviction proceeds: Israel's king is condemned to the death of an outcast, a sinner. Exasperated, Pilate replies, "Take him yourselves and crucify him"—and for a third time declares his innocence. That should be conclusive. But here we are back at the beginning, when Pilate said, "Take him yourselves and judge him according to your law" (18:31). Later, in a different encounter we hear, "We have a law, and by that law he ought to die, because he made himself the Son of God."

This is the heart of the matter. This is why the temple leadership brought Jesus to Pilate in the first place—but John didn't tell us. It is unlikely that Jesus claimed sonship in his lifetime, except, to follow Mark's account, when Caiaphas asked him, "Are you the Messiah, the Son of the Blessed?" (Mark 14:61). Jesus replied, "I am, and you will see the Son of Man seated at the right hand of Power and coming with the clouds of heaven." The High Priest tore his clothes for blasphemy and Jesus was condemned. When Jesus said, "I am—the Son of the Blessed", he was claiming to be the Son of God. He was using the Name, I AM (Exodus 3:14) and, in quoting Daniel 7:13—the Son of Man seated at the right hand of power—he was claiming messianic sovereignty, not only in himself but as the representative of righteous, victorious Israel. When Pilate, therefore, says, "Behold, the man", this means to the temple leadership "The man who said, 'I AM'", who claimed authority as Son of Man, Son of the Blessed, supreme authority on earth and in heaven. No wonder that they shouted "Crucify! Crucify!" with such violence.

Why did John not tell us this earlier? Because it *is* the heart of the matter. It belongs at the climax of his story. That Jesus is the Messiah, the Christ, the Son of God is the faith for which John wrote his book (20:31). The identity of Jesus as Son of God was also the central issue of contention between the church in which John lived and the Jewish synagogues which had probably excluded the followers of Jesus Messiah from membership (9:34-38). This contention underlies much of what John wrote and is responsible for so much of what makes John's Gospel so different from the other three.

Finally, therefore, let us hear again their condemnation of Jesus: "We have a law, and by that law he ought to die, because he made himself the

Son of God." "We have a law": they mean the law of blasphemy—Leviticus 24:16. The law, then, condemns to die him whom Christians confess to be the Son, the embodiment of God. The person or the law? This is the choice with which John presents us. The Teacher ("Rabbouni!"—20:16) or the Teaching (Torah)? This is the issue between church and synagogue to this day, the followers of both finding in those whom they follow the way of life. The person or the book? This is an issue for some in the Church to this day. John wrote his book in the conviction that, in Jesus, the Word was made flesh or, as the writer to the Hebrews put it, that God who had hitherto spoken by the prophets had, "in these last days spoken to us by a Son" (Hebrews 1:2). To him the scriptures bear indispensable witness, but they may not be put in his place. That would be to make an idol of the book: "We have a law." Do this, and we are in danger of exchanging for a legal rigorism the compassion that is the heart of God.

31

The judge

John 19:8–12 *Thursday in Holy Week, Maundy Thursday*

We have not heard before that Pilate was afraid. Now he is very much afraid. If he is faced by someone claiming to be the Son of God, to whose innocence he has three times testified, Pilate is confronted by an authority different from his own. His neutrality is under further pressure. His efforts to release the prisoner have been futile. What if he is compelled to crucify him, and he is who they say he is?

For a second time, Pilate interviews Jesus in the privacy of the Praetorium. Before, Jesus had spoken of his kingdom—not of this world—and of his witness to the truth—ultimate truth. Now, Pilate asks about his identity: "Where are you from?" Jesus is silent. We hear elsewhere (e.g. Mark 15:5) of Jesus' silence before Pilate in the face of accusation, but this is different. On the one hand, "Jesus of Nazareth" is not a sufficient description of Jesus' identity. Nor is, "I came from God." This is true and has been said many times in the Fourth Gospel. Neither is it, however, sufficient: the Word has been made flesh in this man, born in Bethlehem to a woman of Nazareth in Galilee. So Jesus is silent. But let us look a little deeper. Albeit by his enemies, Jesus has been declared to be Son of God, sharing in God what it is to be God. "Where are you from?" then, is not a question that can be asked of God and receive an answer. In his very silence, Jesus testifies to the truth of where he has come from and whose authority he bears. There is an authority that is characteristically silent.

So Pilate resorts to his own authority, of Rome and of Rome's empire, vested in him; the authority to release or crucify, the judicial power of life and death. Jesus replies in the emphatic language that Pilate had previously used to declare his innocence: "You would have no authority whatever over me, had it not been given you from above. Therefore, he who handed me over to you has the greater sin." Pilate's imperial authority is as nothing in the sight of God, except that Pilate has been given his authority to play a part in God's purpose for the salvation of the world. Jesus, however, has a greater authority, which is to discern sin. This is the power of divine judgement. Pilate is not without sin in this matter. Attempting quite properly to cling to neutrality, he has not decided for the truth. Despite declaring Jesus' innocence and trying to free him, he has not chosen the light and remains in darkness.

Nevertheless, there is one whose sin is greater than Pilate's—"he who handed me over to you", says Jesus. This is not Judas, who handed him over to the temple authorities. Nor is it those who brought him to Pilate and who are still standing outside, demanding his death. "He who handed me over to you" is Caiaphas, from whom Jesus was brought: Caiaphas, the spiritual leader of Israel, who had advised that it was expedient, even profitable, that one man die for the people; Caiaphas, who had heard (according to the other Gospels, in various ways) Jesus' "I AM"—"the Son of the Blessed", and taken it for blasphemy. He has the greater sin in being blind and deaf to the truth.

The tables are turned: the judges are judged. Pilate is judged by him who has authority to release or convict of sin, whose judgement is that of the mind of God. With Pilate is judged the world that he represents: Rome, empire, all human power and authority—civil and military, political and judicial, economic and commercial; an authority whose organization against God is ultimately confirmed in arrogating to itself the power of life and death, to release or to crucify. Caiaphas, too, is judged, and with him the nation that rejects her Messiah and demands his death. Here again is the conviction of the world.

After such an interview, no doubt Pilate did seek to release Jesus. But he finds that his authority is indeed as nothing. On one level, Pilate is an unwitting instrument of God's purpose. On another, his power is exposed as hollow. It is delegated, derived, and can therefore be subverted by appeal to Rome: "If you let this man go, you're no friend of Caesar's!" In other words, "Treason! Wait 'til Caesar hears about this!" We're back to the matter of Jesus' kingship, and its potentially seditious overtones.

Pilate, who stands to lose what authority he has, cannot but give way. Jesus must die.

Now we can see what has happened. The unspoken charge upon which Jesus was brought before Pilate was a political one—the kingship of the Jews. This was buttressed by the charge of blasphemy. The two were, of course, entwined: the claim of messiahship—to be king of the Jews—had enormous religious significance, and Jesus very carefully distinguished the religious from the political—"my kingdom is not of this world"; "I have come to bear witness to the truth." Then, however, the blasphemy charge could be introduced when the political one had failed, because it involved an appeal to a Supreme Authority above that of empire or state.

Religion with politics is a dangerous and potentially incendiary mixture: much better to distinguish them and then relate them appropriately. Religious symbols adapted to a political purpose have enormous power to unite and to divide. To attack those who may be politically "other" on the grounds of their religious beliefs is to threaten their identity at a very deep level indeed. To claim religious freedom in support of what are essentially community traditions confuses the issue. However, this happens the world over. Ever since Constantine made Christianity the religion of the Roman Empire, church has supported state and state has supported church. There have been establishments, constitutional privileges, alliances and concordats. Nor is such entanglement of religion and politics restricted to Christianity. The import of Jesus' cross is that his kingdom is unlike any other, exercised in the "weakness" of suffering love.

Yet there is, as so often, an opposite truth. Jesus' kingdom may not be of this world, but he has brought it into the world, and it involves an authority beyond any the world has seen. This brings its citizens and servants into collision with the powers of this world, who seek either to relegate it to the private sphere or to reject any authority above their own. This is why some of those servants suffer—like their Master—for their witness to the truth, as he said they would.

3 2

The verdict

John 19:13–16 *Good Friday*

John's account of Jesus' trial before Pilate begins with his handing over to the Gentiles on an unspecified *charge*. Pilate, interviewing the *witness*, finds himself convicted by that witness' testimony to the truth. Then, as the *prisoner* is brought out to his accusers, he is seen to reign in his humiliation. Next, the *judge* finds himself judged by an authority greater than any he could possess. Everything is paradox, the opposite of what it seems. The cross turns our values upside down. Now comes the *verdict*.

The verdict marks the culmination, the end of the trial. This is judgement day. Pilate must end his shuttling to-and-fro and come to the decision that he dare not take. The judge sits on his tribunal, the judgement seat. Beside him is Jesus, prisoner and witness. Before him are "The Jews"—the nation as represented by its leaders. Pilate says to them, "Here is your king", not now in mockery. He means it. Jesus is no longer in mock laurel and purple, but in his own clothes, the clothes of which he would be stripped at the cross. For his cross too Pilate would write, "Jesus of Nazareth, the King of the Jews", and refuse to change it. The Governor presents their king to his people, and they roar back, "Away with him! Away with him! Crucify him!" Pilate pushes them, "Crucify *your* king?" He has that power: no power now to release him, but power to crucify. This world's power ultimately rests upon coercion and the things of death. The power of life is given through sacrifice.

"We have no king but Caesar." Now the judgement begins. For Israel, God is her king, as she is his people. Her kings, historically, were a concession, permitted on condition of obedience to God and to his commandments (1 Samuel 12:13–15). For five hundred years since the exile to Babylon, Israel had awaited her king. She was awaiting her king from God, her Messiah. So now, rejecting the king they had condemned for blasphemy, her leaders commit the blasphemy of renouncing their God, breaking the covenant, abdicating their position as God's chosen people under his sovereignty. So they judge themselves. This is a terrible judgement, deeply coloured by John's polemic against the synagogue. But, if John's Gospel is addressed to us who hear it, where do we stand between God and Caesar? To whom is our loyalty when we are compelled to decide? We cannot have God *and* Caesar, God *and* the things of Caesar, God *and* anything else. We cannot render to God what is God's in Caesar's coin, nor render to Caesar what is Caesar's in God's coin (Mark 12:17). When the chips are down, God help us, we have to decide, and as we decide we judge ourselves.

Pilate now hands Jesus over to them to be crucified; not to them, literally—Pilate's soldiers will do it—but to their will. At this point some of the details which John relates fall into place. It is the day before Passover, at about noon—that is, at about the time when the slaughter of lambs begins in the temple. (John works to a different timetable from the other Gospels, for a theological purpose.) John is showing us that, in rejecting their king and their position as the people of God, the nation which represents God to the nations of the world, they are about to kill the Lamb of God, the perfect sacrifice. This is, indeed, the Lamb of God who takes away the sin of the world, his people's sins included; the sinless sacrifice, the once-for-all sacrifice. After Jesus' death, John refers to the day that follows not as Passover, but only as "a sabbath of great solemnity". Israel's central religious festival has been superseded, as her mission to the world is accomplished.

Now for another detail. John calls the place of judgement "The Stone Pavement" or Gabbatha. Jesus is crucified at "The Place of the Skull" or Golgotha. No one truly knows where either of them is, but to focus on location is to miss the point. Gabbatha and Golgotha are to be taken together. What happened at Pilate's tribunal is what happens at the cross. When the temple leadership shout, "Away with him! Away with him!", the primary meaning of the Greek is, "Lift him up! Lift him up!", that is, "Crucify him!" It is not the word that Jesus used of himself—that he must be lifted up from the earth to draw all people to himself. These are the words of his opponents, but through their word, his word, God's word, is fulfilled. The whole terrible scene of blasphemy and betrayal is according to the will of God. In sending his Son to die at the hands of blasphemy and betrayal, God has drained the dregs of blasphemy and betrayal to restore the world to himself. As much as Golgotha, Gabbatha is the place of death, so that Golgotha may be the place of life.

Finally, the verdict: there is none, as there was no charge. Pilate is silent. There cannot be a verdict as he delivers to death a man whose innocence he has affirmed in the strongest terms. The innocent is condemned by silence, as so often they are—by the silence of men and women afraid to raise their voices on behalf of the innocent and against the wrongdoers. We shun the suffering. We shun the cross. Yet, in the silence of the verdict stands the judgement of the world. God does not judge us: we bring judgement on ourselves. The cross of the Son of God is both the judgement of the world and the redemption of the world. The cross is the conviction of the world. It is for us to decide.

The cross of the Son of God

3 3

Naming

John 19:17–22 *Monday in Holy Week*

The story of Jesus' crucifixion is substantially the same in all four Gospels, each evangelist describing it in accordance with his own theology and purpose. John too tells it from his own perspective—that kaleidoscope again—to bring out its inner significance. John wants to show us how Jesus, lifted up on the cross, draws all people to himself, and so to be part of this drawing.

For John, the very act of Jesus' crucifixion proclaims him as king. He does not mention Simon of Cyrene: Jesus carries his own cross. He alone is sufficient for the salvation of the world. John does not describe Jesus' two co-crucified as brigands. Such would hardly be fit company for one who is truly a king. And Jesus is named, in a magnificent title—the sort of inscription emperors had on their tombs. Priestly objections are overruled with imperial authority, now reasserted after conceding the demands for Jesus' crucifixion.

JESUS OF NAZARETH, THE KING OF THE JEWS. Pilate wrote this, says John. He named Jesus. No doubt a scribe did the work, but Pilate was responsible for it. Through his office as Governor, it carries the authority of imperial Rome. It is Pilate's testimony to the man he is crucifying and could not save. It is Pilate's testimony to the man they are crucifying—his soldiers, and the temple leadership whose petition and intimidation have brought about Jesus' death. As imperial edict and testimony it stands and may not be revoked.

Hebrew, Latin and Greek: three languages of universal significance. Hebrew is the language of Israel's scriptures; its Aramaic derivative is the language of the people. Latin is the language of the Roman occupation, of the Empire and imperial power. Greek is the common language of the ancient Near East, the language of philosophy, of trade and commerce, the language of the Gospel. Hebrew and Greek: the languages of the Old Covenant and the New; of the faith of a nation and a faith for the world. Hebrew and Latin: the languages of the law of Sinai and the law of Rome: of the chosen people of God and of what would become the first Christian civilization. Hebrew, the language of a singular people; Latin and Greek, the languages that are at the foundation of what would ultimately become the society of the world.

John adds, as no other evangelist does, that it is Jesus of Nazareth who is King of the Jews. This man, in whom the Word became flesh (1:14), the Son of Man who came down from heaven (3:13), is crucified, raised on a cross to return to where he was before. The incarnation was not complete at his birth. The incarnation is the fullness of the life, rejection and death of him who is the embodiment of God, in the person of his Son. It is this man, Jesus of Nazareth, cast out and crucified, who is of universal significance. It is in his death and resurrection that the doctrine of the incarnation becomes a doctrine of salvation and hope.

This proclamation, however, involves a terrible truth. If it is as King of the Jews that Jesus is crucified, this is a stinging insult to the nation. No wonder her leaders protest! Besides, if he *is* King of the Jews, they, by demanding his death, are guilty of sedition. Their last words to Pilate were, "We have no king but Caesar." The title at Jesus' head confirms that they have indeed rejected their Messiah. They have rejected the hope that sustained the nation and rejected their people's future. "He came to his own, and his own received him not" (1:11). It is a terrible judgement.

And there is more. Rejected he may be, but Jesus is still, by divine appointment, by his birth and by the anointing of his baptism, his people's king. As king he carries his own cross. The nation's representative carries the very symbol of Roman oppression, in punishment and death. Jesus embodies the history of his people—outcast, abused, scorned among the nations; made the victims of their own particular faithfulness to God; scapegoats for the ills of the world. John's Gospel has violent things to say about the Jewish people, and on the lips of Jesus, even if those involved are primarily the temple leadership. But it is as the representative of his people that Jesus dies, put to death by Gentiles. Christian history has not allowed for this.

As the trilingual title above his head implies, Jesus' crucifixion is a universal act: the action of a world that always tried to fasten responsibility for its woes on somebody else; the action of a world which would rather not engage with a truth but dismisses it as a claim, "He said, I am the king of the Jews." This is a world that rejects the embodiment of truth, whose significance was teased out in that first interview with Pilate, for the advancement of our own interests or at the dictates of our fears. This is the world that says, "We have no king but Caesar." Pilate's proclamation confronts us all: JESUS OF NAZARETH, THE KING OF THE JEWS—crucified.

3 4

Shaming

John 19:23–25a *Tuesday in Holy Week*

When the soldiers crucified Jesus, they stripped him. Our clothes are not merely protective; they are part of who we are, as people. To be stripped is to be deprived of our personhood, dehumanized, reduced to a body. It was all part of the shame of crucifixion. Jesus' clothes became the soldiers' property. All the Gospels mention that they shared them out, but John goes into detail. The soldiers divide up Jesus' outer garments, and cast lots for his tunic, worn next to the skin. John quotes Psalm 22:18 as being exactly fulfilled in this event. He sees it as of great significance and scholars have debated what he meant.

Some have seen in the seamless tunic an allusion to the robe of a high priest. That, however, was an outer garment, and John never mentions Jesus as a priest. Indeed, the whole religious system of Israel—temple, priesthood and sacrifice—is superseded in Jesus' death. Jesus is the Son, the Word made flesh, a universal figure. Others have seen the tunic as a symbol of the Church's unity—but in the hands of soldiers? John makes the case for unity much better in the great prayer of chapter 17 and in the unbroken fishing net of chapter 21 (21:11; contrast Luke 5:6).

The Gospels of Mark and Matthew tell us that, at the moment of Jesus' death, the veil of the temple was torn in two from top to bottom (Matthew 27:51; Mark 15:38). Luke says that this occurs at the onset of darkness at noon, about three hours before Jesus' death (Luke 23:45). This was the curtain that closed off the sanctuary, the "holy of holies", the innermost shrine of the temple, which the high priest entered once a year, carrying an animal's blood to atone for the sins of Israel. John includes none of this. Instead, he writes of Jesus' tunic, woven from the top throughout, preserved untorn when it is taken from his body. John is showing us the unveiling of the new sanctuary—Jesus' body, crucified.

John tells his story differently from the other Gospels. He places Jesus' cleansing of the temple in his first visit to Jerusalem, at the beginning of his ministry (2:13-22). Challenged about his authority for doing this, Jesus replies, "Destroy this temple, and in three days I will raise it up." His word for "temple" does not mean the whole complex but the sanctuary, the inner shrine. John adds, "He was speaking of the sanctuary of his body." A temple is a meeting place between God and humanity, where God's presence dwells, where worship, prayer and sacrifice are offered, and sin atoned for. By his action in the temple, Jesus declared it redundant. Now its replacement is unveiled—his body, himself, lifted up on the cross to draw all people to himself. He, scourged, condemned, stripped and crucified is now the meeting place of God with all humanity. In this, in him, God has come down to us. This is the place of encounter, of atonement and of worship. The new temple is unveiled precisely by those representatives of "all men" whom Jesus will draw to himself: Pilate's soldiers, the servants and representatives of the power and violence of this world.

What, then, of Jesus' outer garments, which he had laid aside to wash his disciples' feet not twenty-four hours earlier? The very "laying aside" is evocative of Jesus' laying down his life. Now the soldiers divide them. John says, however, only that "they made four parts, to each soldier a part". Four parts: four quarters of a whole. Jesus will gather his elect, as he says in Mark (13:27) "from the four winds, from the ends of the earth to the ends of heaven". Dying, he will, indeed, draw all people to himself.

Now, the moment of which Jesus has already spoken has come (12:23; 13:31-32), in which he is "glorified" and God is "glorified" in him. "Glory" is that which God is, the unknowable presence in the absolute darkness in the innermost shrine at the heart of the temple. Now the glory is unveiled. God, as God is, is revealed in the crucified body of Jesus of Nazareth, the king of the Jews. (King and temple always went together. The temple was a royal foundation. Now they are one.) John says nothing of Jesus' transfiguration. Rather, he tells of the glory revealed, not on a mountain in garments glistening white, but in their removal, at the Place of the Skull. The glory is revealed in the body of Jesus, stripped, dehumanized and crucified; his dying the ultimate revelation of God in him; his death the fulfilment of the Father's will as of his own. This is the truth to which he came to bear witness. Here is the Word made flesh, given for the life of the world.

Here we worship: not on mountains or in temples (4:20-21), but at the cross where Jesus draws us to himself. All true worship is at this place and brings us to this place. Here we worship in spirit and in truth, having no glory of our own. Here we meet him in his crucified nakedness, the mirror of our own. Here our prayer is offered to the Father in the Spirit, through him as he offers himself. This is the place of atonement for us, of our meeting with God. The inaccessible darkness at the heart of the temple, forbidden to all but the high priest, is opened to us in Jesus' death. To come to the cross, however he draws us, is to be drawn into this darkness, but to find in it, in our dying and letting go, the way of life and light and peace.

On the cross, there hung a human body. Henceforth, the human body is to be reverenced as the dwelling place of God; God is to be known in the human body and in the community of human bodies. The incarnation continues in us. We who are in Christ both inhabit "the temple of his body" (2:21) and are that temple, as he abides in us and we in him. Both the human heart and the community of faith are the places in which Christ makes himself known and in which he is discovered. Our coming to faith and our journeys of faith, individually and collectively, are a dis-covering of him in us, an unveiling of the sanctuary within. The unveiling happens as we come to him, walk with him, abide in him and are cleansed and healed by him. It happens especially when we gather to remember, to celebrate, to make present his death for us; to receive him in his enduring humanity in the means that he gave us. Within, of course, is the last place that we look. But the community of faith endures only because he is at its heart. And the human heart redeemed, the heart of stone that has become the heart of flesh (Ezekiel 11:19), is the throne of love.

3 5

Mocking

John 19:25b–27　　　　　　　　　*Wednesday in Holy Week*

Jesus has been crucified and his clothes shared out. Now comes the mockery. The story is familiar: the jeering crowds, the priests pleased with their work, the men crucified with him joining in. John tells nothing of this. They jeered at him as one who was to destroy the temple and build it in three days. John has given us his answer instead: here is the temple of his body, filled with the glory of God, unveiled for those with eyes to see. Mockery has no place in temple precincts. Instead, there is silence: the silence of worship and silence in suffering.

In a temple you would expect to find worshippers—and here they are: his mother and his mother's sister, Mary the wife of Clopas and Mary Magdalene. The four soldiers were Gentiles, unconscious agents of the will of God. Here are four women, Jews, who have remained faithful. John names them, much as the other Gospels do. Mark, however, records that they stood at a distance. John brings them near. They have stood by Jesus as his disciples, even in John's account, have not. So now John brings them into the presence of their Lord. They are a little Christian community, worshipping at the cross; the first of those whom Jesus, lifted up from the earth, has drawn to himself, the forerunners of the whole Church and of every worshipping community.

Mark and Matthew, in fact, name three women watching at the cross. John adds Jesus' mother and "the disciple whom he loved". Neither of them is named, as neither is throughout this Gospel. How is it that they are here when the other Gospels are unambiguous that Jesus' disciples forsook him and fled?

Jesus' mother hardly figures in Jesus' ministry. In Mark, Jesus disavows her: "Whoever does the will of God is my brother and sister and mother" (Mark 3:35). In John, she appears once, at the wedding at Cana of Galilee. It is she who brings to Jesus' attention that the wine has run out. He replies, "Woman, what have I to do with you? My hour has not yet come" (2:4). This looks like another rejection. This, however, was a wedding banquet, a symbol to Israel of the coming of her Messiah. When Jesus' mother says, "They have no wine", she means that the life has gone out of the party. The life has gone out of Israel's faith; the five great stone water jars are empty. "My hour has not yet come." Jesus, Israel's bridegroom, in whom is life, is there but unrecognized. Only through his death, his hour, can his people's life be restored. Only in his dying can he be recognized. Now, however, his "hour" has come. His death gives life to the world. Here he is, the true bridegroom. And his bride? Faithful Israel, represented by that little group of women, his mother included.

Who, too, is the beloved disciple, who appears mysteriously by the cross, faithful after even Peter had failed, and who had been beside Jesus at the supper? He was almost certainly the father-figure of the Christian community that produced this remarkable Gospel. He is a witness of events of profound significance in Jesus' death. Tradition has identified him with John, son of Zebedee. He may, however, be identified with Nathanael, the disciple whose name only appears in the Fourth Gospel, and whose call is unparalleled in the others.* When he saw him, Jesus called him, "a true Israelite, in whom is no deceit" (1:47). He whom Jesus then saw under the fig tree (1:48) is now seen under his cross. *Then* Jesus said to him, "You shall see heaven opened and the angels of God ascending and descending upon the Son of Man" (1:51). Nathanael would see Jesus as Jacob had seen Bethel, with its "ladder", as the house of God and the gate of heaven. Here he is: Jesus, crucified, the new temple; and Jesus, crucified, the meeting place of heaven and earth, of God and humankind—and the beloved disciple is there to see it.

---

* For this identification, I am indebted to an unpublished paper for a Postgraduate Study Day at the University of Exeter, 26 June 1996, by David Catchpole, "Nathanael and the Beloved Disciple".

"Woman, behold your son"; "Behold, your mother." Jesus brings them together. "And from that hour the disciple took her into his own home". This is a perfectly feasible translation of the Greek and shows Jesus providing for his mother. John, however, may have intended to convey something more. He took her, literally, "to his own" (cf. 1:11)—to those things, perhaps, which he owed to Jesus—his faith, discipleship and intimacy with the Lord. As the father-figure of his Christian community, the beloved disciple here represents the Church, the community of faith, and its life sustained by the Spirit. Jesus' mother represents the Israel which gave birth to Jesus, the Israel of Abraham, Isaac and Jacob, of the law and the prophets; the people of God of the covenant fulfilled in Jesus. The disciple represents the people of the new covenant, begun in him. Jesus brings them together. The new covenant embraces the faithful of the old. The old is the seedbed of the new. The seed is Jesus.

The antipathy between the local Jewish community and the Christian community for which John wrote his Gospel is painfully clear in the text. Seeing themselves as the heirs of Israel, the Christian community could paint their opponents as apostate, as they did. There is, however, another side. The immense riches of Jesus' Jewish inheritance, all that his mother represents, have been conferred upon the Church by him (cf. Romans 9:4–5). We, by grace, are the heirs to the spiritual riches of Israel. We have taken for granted what is a divine gift and an enormous privilege.

Finally, having named him, let us restore the beloved disciple's anonymity. John intended that he should be anonymous. He stands for any and every disciple, born of water and the Spirit, called to intimacy with Jesus and beloved of him who has no favourites. To us, then, Jesus says, "Behold, your mother", the mother who said to the servants at Cana, "Do as he tells you." His mother directs us in the way of obedience, to that unity of will with him which he shares with the Father and which brought him to the cross. His mother points us to Jesus, in flesh and blood, in the reality of every day, even when, perhaps, it seems that the wine has run out, and says, "Do as he tells you." Jesus' mother and the beloved disciple are not named precisely because it is their role to point, testify, witness to Jesus—crucified.

3 6

Offering

John 19:28–30   *Thursday in Holy Week, Maundy Thursday*

Jesus hangs upon the cross—JESUS OF NAZARETH, THE KING OF THE JEWS—the representative of his people and the victim of human sin. The Son of God, at once humiliated in death and uplifted in majesty, replaces the temple as the place of encounter with God, to draw all people to himself. In him are joined the people of the first covenant and the new. The work is finished—almost.

One thing remains. Mark tells of the terrible howl of a man forsaken, abandoned by God, which provokes the onlookers into offering him wine. John sees this from the opposite perspective, of the working out of God's sovereign purpose in which men and women are unconscious actors. The sovereign hangs upon the cross. His people may have put him there, but sovereign he remains, inseparable from the Father's will. For the Father's purpose to be fulfilled, one more thing is necessary and Jesus must do it. "I thirst", he says, as when they came to arrest him, he said, "The cup that the Father has given me, shall I not drink it?" Jesus longs to finish the work.

They fill a sponge with sour wine and put it upon a branch of hyssop. Hyssop is the little blue-flowered shrub, whose leaves are the bitter herbs of Passover, with which the Passover Lamb was eaten. The same little shrub was used, two thousand years before, to smear the doorposts and lintel of the Israelites' houses with the lambs' blood that first Passover night. As Jesus hangs upon the cross, the Passover lambs are being slaughtered in the temple in the city. Here, however, is the Lamb of God, proclaimed by the Baptist as he pointed him out at the beginning of his ministry: the Lamb provided by God, as Abraham once promised to sacrifice Isaac. Like Isaac, he carried the wood of the sacrifice himself. At that first Passover, the lambs redeemed the firstborn of Israel, and the people went free. Now, the firstborn dies—the firstborn of God and the firstborn of his people—that they may be free for ever. The king offers himself. In him king, temple and sacrifice are one. The first covenant is complete. Scripture is fulfilled. There is nothing more to be done.

The significance of all this, however, is not exhausted. Passover is celebrated with a sweet wine. Here, however, is sour wine, one jar full of it. This is the drink of soldiers, and they are Gentiles. They put it to his mouth for him to drink: the sour wine of the sin of the world. Jesus drinks his cup to the dregs. This is the new Passover that surpasses the old. This is the Lamb of God who takes away the sin of the world. This is the Passover of the new covenant, the forgiveness of sins. As temple and sacrifice in Jesus are one, so he is the propitiation, the atoning sacrifice for the sins of the whole world. What the high priest did for Israel annually, with animal blood in the darkness at the heart of the temple, Jesus does himself, openly, outside the city, once for all. He offers himself. The Lamb gives his flesh for the life of the world.

Now it is done. The work is finished—the Father's work which he gave Jesus to do (4:34). The world is reconciled to God. The way is open for all who will receive him (1:12) to become children of God. Jesus has given himself completely. God in him has given everything. In him, God has given everything. Nothing is withheld. This is the extremity of abandonment out of which Jesus cried. It is also, in this very giving of everything, the ultimate embodiment of the glory of God. "It is finished." In a gesture of obedience which sums up the whole, Jesus bows his head and gives up his spirit.

3 7

Piercing

John 19:31–37 *Good Friday*

"It is finished." The Lamb of God has offered himself for the sin of the world. Could more possibly be said? John has more to say. He tells of a move to break the legs of those who were crucified, and of Jesus' bones preserved unbroken. He records eyewitness testimony to a flow of blood and water from a spear thrust into Jesus' side. He repeats again that scripture is fulfilled. This is a passage full of difficulties. The other Gospels are silent about it all, except that a soldier confessed faith in the crucified. And this, perhaps, is the key to it. Here we are concerned with the response to the cross, a response that brings to a head the great themes of the whole of the Fourth Gospel: faith or unbelief; sight or blindness; salvation or judgement; life or death. Had not Jesus said (9:39), "For judgement I came into this world, so that those who do not see may see, and that those who see may become blind"?

The temple leadership returns to Pilate to request the removal of the bodies of the crucified men before the Sabbath. This is a scrupulous observance of Deuteronomy 21:22–23, but it is an unflattering scene. Their request for the breaking of legs implicates them again in a punishment that would have been considered abhorrent. There is, perhaps, an echo of that legalism which said, "We have a law, and by that law he ought to die." Again, the portrait has been coloured by the conflict between church and synagogue. There is here, however, the universal opposition of blindness and faith. To those who request the breaking of legs, Jesus is one of three crucified men. They have not recognized their king, the Lamb of God, nor his completion of the Passover. Indeed, their request that his legs be broken is an unconscious violation of their law, that no bone of the

Passover lamb should be broken (Exodus 12:46; Numbers 9:12). In their eyes, Jesus is, indeed, "numbered among the transgressors". The charge of spiritual blindness levelled against Israel's leaders throughout the Gospel has reached its climax in a terrible irony. It is the righteous servant of the Lord who is "numbered among the transgressors" (Isaiah 53:12), as it is also the righteous man who is kept by the Lord, "so that not one of his bones is broken" (Psalm 34:20). Israel's leaders, however, cannot see him. John drives home the point by referring to the Passover, on whose eve Jesus has been crucified only as "the sabbath", albeit of "great solemnity". In John's narrative, the salvific event of Passover has lost its meaning for them. It is, again, a terrible judgement.

The blindness is also on the side of religion: religion that will countenance inhumanity and cruelty in defence of its tenets. This is not a judgement on an unbelieving world. The cross brings division, as Jesus brought division throughout his ministry, but the judgement does not fall where we might expect it. The danger facing religious people is that we claim to know the unknowable and to "see" the invisible, but we are blind to the Lord when he comes in flesh and blood. It is by our response in this situation that we are judged—or, rather, that we judge ourselves.

To blindness, John opposes a testimony of faith: that from the spear thrust into Jesus' side by one of Pilate's soldiers there flowed blood and water. By this he indicates that something wonderful and extraordinary has happened, confirming all the themes of temple and sacrifice that faith sees fulfilled in Jesus. In the theology of the day, life was in the blood; we speak of lifeblood still. When an animal was sacrificed its blood was poured out as its life was offered in support of the petitioner's prayer. The blood flowing from the crucified body of Jesus, therefore, is evidence of the life that flows from him. He has said of his blood that it is "drink indeed" (6:55), truly life-giving to those who receive it. He had spoken, too, of living water flowing from the belly of those who would believe in him, as a promise of the Spirit (7:38-9). If Jesus, crucified, is indeed the new temple, the meeting place of God and humankind, the flood of life-giving water from the temple in Ezekiel's vision (Ezekiel 47:1-12) comes immediately to mind. That water flowed from the south side of the temple, grew deeper the further it went, and brought life wherever it went, even to the Dead Sea. This, then, is the water of life, the life of the resurrection, the life that renews all life, flowing from the side of the crucified Jesus, the "living water" promised to the woman of Samaria (4:10,14). This "testimony" of the disciple who saw it is a vision of life: life for the world, flowing from the crucified Christ, who is himself the source of this life.

To this, again, John couples a scriptural text: "They shall look on him whom they have pierced" (Zechariah 12:10). In its context, this introduces a vision of universal mourning in Jerusalem for one whom they have killed, mourning as if for an only child. Here, however, one of Pilate's soldiers has done the piercing, either a callous act of random violence or to be certain of Jesus' death. The piercing has been done by a Gentile, a servant of imperial power and of the world at large. Against the blindness of religion is offered the possibility of a universal "seeing" of Jesus, a recognition of him whom we have pierced in our participation in the sin of the world, our share in its injustices, our complicity in its cruelties, our failure to recognize him in flesh and blood. It is in repentance and mourning that we avail ourselves of the life which flows from the crucified Christ.

3 8

A burial fit for a king

John 19:38–42 *Good Friday evening*

The story ends with a burial fit for a king. Since he was brought before Pilate, for those with eyes to see, Jesus has been proclaimed as king. Pilate recognizes him and offers the temple leadership the freedom of their king. They choose Barabbas. Pilate's soldiers dress and mock Jesus as king. Pilate produces him as king, robed in purple, crowned with thorns,* and the leaders reject their king. Pilate's judgement proclaims Jesus as king, and the people demand the death of their king. The notice on Jesus' cross declares him as king, and Pilate refuses to change it. Jesus dies as king, his work accomplished, his life fulfilled. Finally, he is buried as king.

A mixture of myrrh and aloes is brought, a hundred pounds in weight: two back-packs full. These are spices, not oils—for Jesus has already been anointed for his burial (12:7). Spices were used in burial to counter the stench of decay (11:39), but this is a lavish, extravagant quantity. This is a testimony of faith. Jesus is being honoured in death as he was not in life. In a brand-new tomb, he is given, in haste, a burial fit for a king.

Jesus is being honoured by people who have until now kept their faith to themselves. This is the effect of martyrdom, of those whose witness to the truth takes them to their death. Joseph of Arimathea was a disciple in secret. Nicodemus first came to Jesus by night (3:1–2). Both have now "come out", gone public; Joseph by going to Pilate for Jesus' body; Nicodemus in producing a half-hundredweight of spices. Has

---

* The symbolism is the more compelling if, indeed, the "thorns" are not the vicious spikes of buckthorn, of medieval piety, but the luscious leaves of Acanthus.

he, perhaps, through Jesus' death, been born anew (3:3), to enter the kingdom of God, through the water that has flowed from his side and the Spirit given in his death (19:30)?

Jesus is buried in a garden. It was, of course, to a garden that Judas came to betray him. There was a garden, says John, in the place where he was crucified. So it is in a garden that Jesus is buried, in which, two days later, Mary Magdalene will stand, weeping, at an empty tomb and thinking that she sees the gardener. So is planted the seed of the new creation. The gardens of betrayal and crucifixion, the places of our sin, become a new Garden of Eden, in which stands the cross, the tree of life (Genesis 2:9), no longer inaccessible but available to all. Nor was Mary mistaken. He is the Gardener.* The Garden is his creation. The leaves of the tree are for the healing of the nations (Revelation 22:2). The kingdom has come. The new creation has come to birth. In Christ the King is the hope for the world.

---

* I am indebted for this insight to Margaret Daly-Denton, *John: An Earth Bible Commentary* (London: T&T Clark, 2017), pp. 13–26.

3 9

Resurrection faith

John 20:1–2; 11–18   *Easter Day*

Mary Magdalene came to the tomb as a mourner. It was as dark outside the tomb as inside, and as dark inside herself. Mary loved Jesus deeply. She had been there at his cross. All four Gospels say so. Like any mourner she goes to where his body lies. That is where "he" is. The reality that "he" is not here is too painful to bear. Mary is without hope. "The Lord", she calls him, but her Lord is dead. With him, part of herself has died, the only part that matters at that moment. She finds the stone removed. She knows that his body is gone, and that she must find it. Her grief is that of everyone who has lost the one dearest to them in all the world. The anguish of not knowing where "he" is would be our own.

Mary is representative of us in another way too. She was not alone at the cross: two or three other women, at least, were with her (19:25), the first little Christian community gathered around the cross of their Lord. In the other Gospels, they accompany her on her early morning pilgrimage. She speaks for them all in saying, "We do not know where they have laid him."

If Mary had expected comfort from the two to whom she told her news, she found none. After their visit, she stands weeping. Through her tears she peeps into the tomb, its darkness and emptiness the mirror of her own. But the darkness is lit by the angels of God's presence. In the darkness, the emptiness, God is present and at work. Israel knew this: the temple had at its heart the absolute darkness of its most holy place. Now it is the tomb that has become the place of divine activity. Jesus has lain there, and the divine presence begins to prepare her to meet her Lord. The angels invite her to speak her grief, the first step in setting free. The first glimmer of dawn breaks within Mary as she speaks for herself: "They have taken away my Lord, and I do not know where they have laid him."

It is enough: Jesus has heard and he is here. As she turns to him, unknowing, he takes the initiative. He was sovereign in crucifixion: he is sovereign still. He too invites her to speak her grief—"Woman, why are you weeping?"—but he adds, "Whom are you looking for?" Look, not for a body but for a person. Mary hardly hears him. She speaks of taking possession of his body. But, very gently, Jesus is breaking the deadlock of her grief, bringing her to the point when she can hear her name, "Mary!"

Light floods her darkness! Jesus' presence fills her emptiness. This is the moment of resurrection as Mary is raised from her grief. This is the moment of faith in which we find ourselves known, named and loved by him who fills all creation. Mary turns to him again, turning in heart and soul to her Lord. This is her conversion. She responds in Hebrew,* the divine language of Israel, we might almost say "in tongues"—"Rabbouni!"—a form of Rabbi used in address to God. Jesus has brought Mary from death to life, the Lord who died for her. So of course she clings to her beloved, to prolong for ever this moment of inexpressible joy! But Mary must let go. They cannot be as once they were, disciple and rabbi, pupil and teacher. That relationship belongs to the old life. Mary must move on, in faith, and let him go. Faith is not faith if in our mind we detain Jesus in this world. Do this, and we make an idol of Jesus, as one of us. It is as if, in meeting Mary, Jesus has broken his journey to the Father to bring her, and all who hear her testimony, to understand what faith is. Faith is in God, or it is not faith at all. Even on Easter Day, we must look beyond the risen Jesus. If Jesus is to command our faith and obedience, he must be ascended, united with God, indwelling the Father, as sovereign, Lord. Faith looks not to Jesus, but to Jesus in the Father, or to the Father through Jesus. Speaking to his disciples through Mary, Jesus calls them "my brothers". Jesus has no children. Through him, we are all children of God.

When Mary took Jesus' message to the disciples, she prefaced it with her testimony: "I have seen the Lord." Testimony carries conviction.

---

* A note to the NRSV translation at this point says, pedantically, "that is, Aramaic". John wrote "in Hebrew" and knew what he meant!

Testimony authenticates the message, whether we have "seen" the Lord in scripture (which is why John wrote his Gospel (20:31)) or in mystical experience; whether we have heard his voice in prayer, felt his hand in healing or accepted his call to service. In all these ways we share in his resurrection as Mary Magdalene did. Her testimony, too, is his word to a church that has died: that is gathered around his cross and honours him as crucified but doesn't know him risen. The risen Lord gives life and bestows the Spirit. The risen Lord gathers his people and leads his Church. The risen Lord speaks and calls, heals and saves. If we have the risen Christ in our midst as we celebrate, our hope cannot be shaken, our confidence is secure and our joy will be complete.

4 0

The new temple

John 20:1–18 *Easter Day*

Two men running. The tomb of the man to whom they had committed their lives was empty. One, the closer to Jesus, on his right at their last meal together two nights before, ran faster and arrived first. He saw the broad linen strips in which the body had been wound; the body is gone. The second, Peter, goes further and enters the tomb. The cloths are lying orderly, undisturbed, coverings of head and body separate. They haven't been unwound. No question of theft, of robbery or resuscitation. The first disciple enters, sees it all, and comes to life. He is not *here*, but he IS!

And Mary Magdalene? Mary is looking for the man she loves. She never speaks of his body—always, "the Lord", "my Lord", or "him". In her grief it is, perhaps, too soon to distinguish. Mary's is, however, the language of faith, of seeking the Lord. Mary speaks for us, outside that empty tomb. When she turns and seems *him*, he is not as she expects. He cannot be. His gentle question draws her out—her longing, her faith— and then he can reveal himself. He must reveal himself because, until that moment of delight, Mary cannot see *him*. He has died. He is changed. He comes disguised as someone else. Even then, she must let him go.

The empty tomb declares the resurrection an act of God—through which Jesus has transcended the boundaries of existence, and lives. His meeting with Mary declares that he who is risen now reigns as Lord, the Lord whom we seek. At that moment in history when touch might have been possible, Mary must not do so. She cannot possess him. We have to let him go, to be himself, to be him who always is: to reign as Lord. Only if he ascends to the Father, who always is, can he be the Lord of our lives, of our prayers, of our beginning and our end.

And the angels in the tomb? They manifest the divine presence, and they are "sitting one at the head and one at the feet where the body of Jesus was lying". Except that it was no longer there! The religious imagination recalls the cherubim of the temple in the holy of holies, at each end of the ark of the covenant. Here, then, in the undisturbed graveclothes, is the "ark" of the new covenant, the symbol of God's presence among his people. So the tomb—the "new tomb in which no one had ever been laid" (19:41)—betokens the new temple, of Jesus' body, built in three days. The stone rolled away proclaims the temple as his body—risen—the person, not the place. The sequence begun in Gabbatha and Golgotha ends in "Rabbouni!" It is in Jesus the Lord that God is to be found: the Lord whom we seek. As he said to Mary, "Whom are you looking for?"

If, too, we may follow through the moment when the soldiers' disposal of Jesus' clothing marks the unveiling of God's glory in his dying body, the removal of the stone, whose placing John does not record, marks the moment when the glory—which is the body of Jesus—returns to the glory of the Father from whom he came.

All this happens in a garden. John alone tells of a garden "in the place where Jesus was crucified". John tells of Jesus' betrayal, death, burial and resurrection all happening in gardens. There is more here than a parallel with the Garden of Eden. Gardens were walled. If, therefore, the tomb represents the new temple, the garden represents the temple court, where Jesus walks (10:23) and may be found. And the garden is a place of civilization, in which we build upon nature. Gardens express our partnership with nature at its best. Gardens are productive. Gardens are sustainable. Gardens represent the way we must learn to live on this planet. Gardens are places of order and beauty. Gardens are for living in. Gardens are places of peace and peacefulness, rest, enjoyment, Sabbath ... The garden, therefore, is a symbol of the new creation and of life in the hands of Jesus, the Gardener. The community around us is his garden, of which he is the Gardener. We are to work with him in it, so that it may be productive, peaceful, restful, beautiful—a place of God's presence, a place of salvation. Otherwise, there is only that other garden—of betrayal—in which our sin is exposed.

We live in a garden. We must come to the tomb. This is the pattern of our life. But in this garden, the tomb bears the promise of eternal life in the presence of Jesus Christ, crucified and risen, reigning in the glory of the Father, our Lord.

Bibliography

Brown, Raymond E., SS, *The Death of the Messiah: A Commentary on the Passion Narratives in the Four Gospels* (London: Geoffrey Chapman, 1994).

Barrett, C. K., *The Gospel according to St John* (second edition, London: SPCK, 1978).

Bauckham, Richard, *Jesus and the Eyewitnesses: The Gospels as Eyewitness Testimony* (Grand Rapids, MI: Wm. B. Eerdmans, 2006).

Caird, G. B., *The Gospel of St Luke* (London: A & C Black, 1968).

Daly-Denton, Margaret, *John: An Earth Bible Commentary* (London: T&T Clark, 2017).

Evans, C. F., *Saint Luke* (London: SCM Press, 1990).

Fenton, J. C., *The Gospel of St Matthew* (Harmondsworth: Penguin Books, 1963).

Gundry, Robert H., *Mark: A Commentary on His Apology for the Cross* (Grand Rapids, MI: Wm. B. Eerdmans, 1993).

Gundry, Robert H., *Matthew: A Commentary on His Handbook for a Mixed Church under Persecution* (second edition, Grand Rapids, MI: Wm. B. Eerdmans, 1994).

Harrington, Wilfred, OP, *Mark* (Dublin: Veritas, 1979).

Hooker, Morna D., *The Gospel according to St Mark* (London: A & C Black, 1991).

Lindars, Barnabas, SSF, *The Gospel of John* (London: Marshall, Morgan & Scott, 1972).

Marsh, John, *The Gospel of St John* (London: Penguin Books, 1968).

Marshall, I. Howard, *The Gospel of Luke: A Commentary on the Greek Text* (Exeter: The Paternoster Press, 1978).

Milner-White, Eric, *My God, my Glory* (London: SPCK, 1954).

Nineham, D. E., *The Gospel of Mark* (London: A & C Black, 1968).

The Church of Ireland, *The Book of Common Prayer* (Dublin: The Representative Body of the Church of Ireland, 2004).

EU GPSR Authorized Representative:

LOGOS EUROPE, 9 rue Nicolas Poussin, 17000 La Rochelle, France

contact@logoseurope.eu

www.ingramcontent.com/pod-product-compliance
Lightning Source LLC
Chambersburg PA
CBHW070555160426
43199CB00014B/2507